THE POEMS OF
DR. ZHIVAGO

THE POEMS OF
DR. ZHIVAGO

Translated
with a Commentary
by

DONALD DAVIE

MANCHESTER UNIVERSITY PRESS
BARNES & NOBLE, NEW YORK

© 1965 DONALD DAVIE
Published by the University of Manchester at
THE UNIVERSITY PRESS
316–324 Oxford Road, Manchester, 13

First published
in the United States
in 1965 by
BARNES & NOBLE, INC
Publishers, Booksellers, founded 1873
105 Fifth Avenue
New York, 3

Printed in Great Britain by Butler & Tanner Ltd
Frome and London

The Translator and the Publishers acknowledge the permission of Messrs. William Collins Sons and Co. Ltd. for the right to publish a new translation of the poems in *Dr. Zhivago*. To them also the translator is grateful for permission to quote extensively from the translation of *Dr. Zhivago* by Manya Harari and Max Hayward. To Giangiacomo Feltrinelli Editore we are also grateful for allowing us to reproduce photographically the Russian text of the poems.

CONTENTS

INTRODUCTION

At the end of Pasternak's *Doctor Zhivago*, translated by Max Hayward and Manya Harari, there appear, in the British edition, 25 pieces under the heading, 'Zhivago's Poems'. The reader does not know what to do with these pages; we are given no indication of how they are connected with the 464 pages of prose narrative which precede them, and as soon as we begin to read this enigmatic appendix we find it as wearisome as reading verse in prose translation usually is.

I have set out to discover what function Pasternak intended these pages to serve, how he intended us to read them, and how they are connected with what goes before them. I believe I have found that unless we read these poems in the right way we have failed to read *Doctor Zhivago* at all; that, contrary to appearances, *Doctor Zhivago* is not a novel with an appendix of poems, but one whole thing, intricately interlocking, in which prose supports poetry and vice versa; that the many discussions whether *Doctor Zhivago* is a good novel, or a true novel, are all beside the point so long as Zhivago's poems are considered an optional appendix, or bonus, to something which can stand without them.

The first requirement was to translate Zhivago's poems afresh; and the translations which follow are the versions I made. That is to say, they are working translations: the whole point in making them was to cleave very closely and faithfully to the original, to

1

bring over all the sense of the Russian, and to introduce nothing that the Russian gives no warrant for. There could be no question in this case of imitation, adaptation, paraphrase, so-called 'free' translation. (To this there is one exception, the 9th poem in the sequence; see my note to that poem.) Nevertheless, these are *verse*-translations, as they have to be if faithfulness is what we are after. To quote D. G. Rossetti:

The life-blood of rhythmical translation is this commandment: that a good poem shall not be turned into a bad one. The only motive of putting poetry into a fresh language must be to endow a fresh nation, if possible, with one more possession of beauty.

'If possible . . .' And of course it is not possible always, nor even very often; yet this must always be the objective that is aimed at.

I should like to be more specific. For it is commonly believed that a translation, if it is close, cannot be poetic; or if it is poetic, cannot be close. Yet why be surprised if it is poets who offer the closest translations? It is their business and also their passion to know what poetry is, wherein it consists. It is for instance the professional poet who knows that in the end rhyme and metre (though certainly not rhythm) are normally expendable; that neither the substance of poetry nor the *form* of poetry are to be found in these features—that on the contrary the essential form is the track of the poet's feeling, from first to last through his poem. There are exceptions; poems in which rhyme for instance plays an unusually vital role. The third of Zhivago's poems is such an exception, and I have given it exceptional treatment. But in general the verse-translator who is a professional poet will realize that in translating rhymed verse the rhyme is the first thing to go, and metre the second; whereas the amateur, wretched sceptic that he is, cannot be sure of having poetry at all unless he has these external features of it.

I have supplied notes to each poem; and these are designed to hang together in a continuous commentary on the form and significance of *Doctor Zhivago* as a whole, as this has emerged for me through translating the poems and re-reading the prose. Here I will briefly state in advance the conclusions I have reached.

The poems are faithful to a psychological reality, the psychological reality of poetic composition in the act of dredging up, transforming, and juxtaposing memories. One of the pleasures which they provide is of the kind that we get from J. Livingstone Lowes's book about Coleridge, *The Road to Xanadu*; we see the poet (Zhivago, not Pasternak) dealing magisterially with the images which we have seen him accumulate throughout his life. The sixteen chapters of prose narrative present us with the life; the seventeenth chapter, of poems (for this is the arrangement in the Russian edition), presents the art which came out of that life, its crown and its justification. If we try to justify Zhivago's life without taking his poems into account, we shall fail. For the justifications which we shall then find will not be those which Pasternak intended, or would accept. Many of the poems draw for images on widely separated and logically unconnected parts of Zhivago's life as we know it from the novel; and conversely many passages of the prose have no function, and no place in the economy of the whole, except that they can be seen to present Zhivago with images which later get into one of his poems.

From this point of view, the best hint on how to read the poems is early in the novel, in the first section of Chapter Three, which tells how Zhivago's mother-in-law contracted the illness which was to prove fatal. She slipped when assisting the handyman to install an antique wardrobe:

Anna did not like the wardrobe. Its shape and size reminded her of a catafalque or a royal tomb and filled her with a superstitious dread. She nicknamed it the tomb of Askold; she meant the horse of Prince Oleg, which had caused its master's death. Owing to her unsystematic reading her association of ideas was odd.

After this incident Anna developed a pulmonary weakness.

One shudders to think of the symbol-hunting critic (some have been at work on *Doctor Zhivago* already) who will take note of this, and will notice also that, twenty pages later, when Anna's coffin is being carried out of her room, the handyman 'got stuck in the bedroom where the wreaths had been piled up, because the bedroom door was blocked by that of the wardrobe on the landing, which had swung open' (the 16th section of Chapter Three). The same wardrobe! What allegories one would be meant to read into this, if *Doctor Zhivago* had been written by Hawthorne! But in Pasternak's novel I take it that, if there is anything to this incident beyond the pathos and the irony which chance introduces into all our lives, it represents as it were a poem offered to Zhivago which he never got round to writing. 'Owing

4

to her unsystematic reading her association of ideas was odd'—so is Zhivago's, so is everyone's; and of absorbing interest to Pasternak is this oddity, and the logic which lies hidden in and behind it.

I do not intend, by thus stressing the psychological interest in *Doctor Zhivago*, to deny or minimize the metaphysical and religious interests which Pasternak seems to pursue. He truly does pursue them; and if the metaphysical references can be translated into psychological terms (Jesus the Redeemer being scaled down into Zhivago the Poet), so the psychological interests are metaphysical also, and the Poet truly is the Redeemer. For what Pasternak knows about the poet's mind and how it works creatively is not just part of what he knows about the human mind; it is also part of what he knows about purpose in the universe, and about the mind of God. Thus, when John Strachey, in his interesting and valuable essay, 'The Strangled Cry', says that Pasternak in *Doctor Zhivago* sets up three ultimate values, Love, Art and Christ, what needs to be said is that these three values are for Pasternak not distinct. These are three aspects of one reality, which can be approached through experience of God, through experience of woman, or through experience of art—the experience of creating art, not (I think) the experience of appreciating it.

The approach we follow in *Doctor Zhivago* is the experience of creating art. Far more than it is a love-story, *Doctor Zhivago* is the story of an artistic vocation. On top of the experience of appreciating art which *Doctor Zhivago* offers since it is itself a work of art, we get from it also the experience of creating art

5

—a vicarious experience certainly, but perhaps none the worse for that.

If I see the book in this way, I cannot easily find a parallel to it. It has been many times observed that if an author introduces into his book a character who is alleged to be brilliantly witty, he is under the necessity of constantly finding brilliantly witty things for that character to say; and similarly the trouble with a fictional character who is alleged to be a greatly endowed artist is that we are inevitably required to take his great gifts on trust—that which gives significance to his life is precisely the one thing about him which cannot be shown, which we can only be told about. This is the trouble with Thomas Mann's *Doctor Faustus*. After all the exertions which Mann takes to establish Adrian Leverkuhn as a great composer of music, in the end we have to take this on trust. Nothing could *prove* this contention short of Mann's providing us with the scores of Leverkuhn's alleged compositions; and for these to match what Mann claims for Leverkuhn, the scores would have to reveal in Mann as great a composer as Arnold Schoenberg—which is absurd. Only in the one art of literature can this difficulty be overcome; and Pasternak, so far as I am aware, is the one writer to have realized this and acted accordingly. It is essential to the meaning of *Doctor Zhivago* that Zhivago should be a great poet. Very well; instead of merely telling us that this is so, Pasternak *proves* it—in the only way possible, that is, by giving to Zhivago great poems. They are not poems by Pasternak which he merely donates to Zhivago, but truly Zhivago's poems in that they can be seen to derive from Yury Zhivago's experience, not from Boris Pasternak's.

THE POEMS TRANSLATED INTO
ENGLISH VERSE

1

HAMLET

The buzz abates. I have issued upon the boards
And I hang on the jamb of a door
To flush from recession of echoes
What the times intend shall occur.

Down all of a thousand opera-glasses'
Axes focused, dark of the night impales me.
Abba, my father, let this cup
Pass from me, if it may be.

I love your stubborn shaping of a theme.
I have agreed to play this character.
But now a different drama is in train.
Leave me this once an unscripted actor.

But the scenes' sequence was thought out
      beforehand,
Not to be evaded is the end they move to.
I am alone, all sinks to the Pharisee.
Living a life is not a field we pass through.

2

MARCH

The sun works up to a lather,
To a thresh in stupefied lowlands.
Like the chores of a strapping cow-girl,
Spring's busy-ness seethes through the hands.

9

Snow sinks, anaemia saps it
Along weak, blue, twig-like veins.
But life smokes up from the cowhouse;
Hale, it darts out from the tines of pitchforks.

All these nights, these days and nights!
Thud of the thaw at noon, the spatter
Of icicles dripping from roof-tops,
The sleepless culverts' chatter . . .

Open it all lies, stable and cowshed.
Pigeons peck oat-ears out of snow.
Off the all-blameable, all-engendering
Dunghill the air blows freshly.

3

IN HOLY WEEK

Still all around night's murk in the air.
Still in the world so soon astir,
Stars in the sky more than any man knew
And each of them, like day, shone true,
And had earth chosen what to do
She would have slept all Easter through
To the sound of the Psalter.

Still all around night's murk in the air.
Life so betimes is come
That, all eternity, the Square
Corner to cross-roads spread out there,
And thence to dawn and warmer air
Stretched a millennium.

The earth is all a barebones yet
And o' nights has never a tatter
To swing on a bell-rope in, and set
Chimes to the chorister.

And from Maundy Thursday
Through to Easter Sunday
Water bores the bank away
Drills in the eddy.

Forests uncover and divest themselves
And at Christ's Passion-tide
Congregated pinestems guide
Order of worship, steadfast.

But in the town the space is straiter
For a poor gathering
Of trees that at the church's grating
Stand stark and peering.

Aghast they gaze. And they have cause,
As may be understood:
No fence holds in the gardens' force,
Earth trembles now through all her course;
They sepulchre a God.
Through the Tsars' Gate they see the light
And the black shroud, and the candles' order,
The faces streaming-eyed—
And abruptly towards them the cross and
    banners
And the blessed grave-cloth ride,
And the two birches at the gateway
Must stir and stand aside.

Round the slow procession paces
Almost in the street,
And back to its courts out of public places
Brings Spring, Spring's gossip, and the traces
Of the Host still tasted in the air's spaces,
And a Spring smell, heady and sweet.

And March spills snow in a sudden scurry
On the church-porch huddle of the maimed
As if there were someone came
And brought and opened a reliquary
And gave away each last straw.

And singing lasts until the dawn
When, tears all spent, more calm
And softlier, from withindoors drawn,
Sounds, over lamplit barrens borne,
The gospel-chant or psalm.

But, mute at midnight, flesh and fur
Hear the Spring's prediction
Murmured, how the seasons stir
And Death may have a vanquisher
By might of Resurrection.

4

WHITE NIGHT

Before me a far-off time arises,
A house in the Petersburg quarter.
Daughter of modest gentry from the Steppes
Is what you are; Kursk-born, attending courses.

You are attractive, boys pursue you.
This white night, we two are
Looking out from your window sill
In a skyscraper, down at the view.

The street-lamps are like butterflies made of gas
Which the morning has touched to a first tremor.
This which I tell you quietly
Is in accord with distances in slumber.

We are caught up in the same confidences
Safeguarded with apprehension,
As in the widespread panorama
Petersburg is, behind Neva's boundless expanses.

There in the distance, in the tangled brakes
On this white spring night
Worshipful thunder of the nightingale
Is released by limits of woodland.

The lunatic trills unroll,
The voice of the small unnoticeable bird
Excites elation and turmoil
In the depths of spellbound thickets.

Towards that place the bare-footed vagrant,
    Night,
Worms his way, inching along by fences;
Behind him from the window sill runs out
A trail of talk, of overheard exchanges.

Within earshot of talk that is shared,
In the garden, in the fenced enclosures
The apple-bearing branches and the cherries
Change into blossom-white dresses.

13

And the spectral trees debouch,
A white throng in the highway,
As if to speed with a gesture
White night that has seen so much.

5

FOUL WAYS IN SPRINGTIME

The fires of sunset burning out, by foul
Footing on quickset forest track,
To a homestead deep in the Urals
Toiled one on horseback.

Jar of his mount's loud teeth upon the bit,
And hard upon the shock-waves of the horse's
Shod hooves spattering, all the way pursuit
Echoed, of springs sluicing down watercourses.

Or when his hold on the reins slackened
And he slowed to a walking pace,
The floods swept by, and followed near at hand,
Grinding and deafening, the water-race.

Someone laughed, someone wept.
Stone crumbled, dashed on stone,
And down the cascades, whirling, swept
Stumps torn out of root-lock, and pitched dowr

But on the burnt-out premises of sundown
And charred black branchy distances, prevail
Like the sullen bell of the tocsin
Fulminations of the nightingale.

Where the widowed willow dips her veil,
Inclined aslant the gully,
There, like the ancient Robber-Nightingale,
He fluted on his sevenfold oak-tree whistle.

What calamity or paramour
Was object of this love?
Whom was that small-shot meant for,
Sprayed from redoubtable barrels across thickets?

It seemed that, look! wood-goblin, he confronted,
Come from the bivouac of the wanted man,
The mounted or else unmounted levies
Of the local Partisan.

Earth and sky, forest and fallow-plot,
Caught that discontinuous strain,
Those portionings out by lot
Of trials, glee, fatuities, and pain.

6

EXPLANATION

Life has come back with as little reason
As once it was strangely interrupted.
I am in the same old-fashioned thoroughfare
Now as then, in the selfsame summer season.

People the same, with the same troubles,
And the fire of sunset no cooler
Since that which death of an afternoon
Nailed up on the Manège's gables.

In the cheap cottons that they always wore
Women still go slopping by at night-time.
After a while, under the iron roofs
The attics crucify them as before.

Here is a tired one, taking the going hard,
Slowly comes out on a doorstep
And, climbing up from a basement,
Goes slanting across the yard.

Once again I get ready excuses
And again I couldn't care less.
And the neighbour goes round by the alley
And leaves us without intrusions.

Don't cry, don't primp into pleats and knit
Your swollen lips in puckers.
You will pick the dried scab open
Over spring's fever-fit.

Take the flat of your hand off my chest.
We are wires, the current through us
—Watch out for it!—has no reason
That again it throws us abreast.

Years will pass, you'll be married before you
   know it,
You'll forget these maladjustments.
It's a great step to take, to be woman;
To unhinge us is quite an exploit.

For me, in fealty I shall bow
Before the miracle of hands or throat,
Shoulder or arm or spine of woman
At every age as now.

16

And yet however night and my cravings may
Weld hoops around me, there's a stronger pull
Still in the world; the Passionate draft pulls
Out for the breakaway.

7

SUMMER IN THE CITY

Muted exchanges and
With a fervid haste
The hair is gathered up,
A whole shock swept from the nape.

From under the heavy comb
Looks out a woman helmed
The head falling
Backward among braids.

Along the street the night
Is close, promising storm
And a break-up comes, a shuffle,
Walkers dispersing homeward.

Abruptly thunder is heard
And its rejoinder, edgy,
And the wind swings
The window-curtain.

Ensues a hush.
As before, closeness.
As before, lightnings
Grope, grope in the heavens.

And when, with the breaking light
The morning, again torrid,
Dries puddled avenues
After nocturnal downpour,

There comes a look that is
Cross-grained from lack of sleep
About the centuries-old,
Fragrant, unfading limes.

8

WIND

This is my end, but you live on.
And the wind, complaining and lamenting,
Agitates forest and country lodge.
Not the pine trees one by one
But a consensus of all trees
And the boundless distances, on and on,
Like hulls that are stripped of canvas
In a haven satin for squadrons.
And this not out of audacity
Nor from a fury without occasion,
But in anguish to find you
Words for a cradle-song.

9

BARLEY-MOW

Under the broom here, ivy-clad,
The squall sends us to cover.
We hunch our shoulders under the plaid,
My hands on you ivying over.

18

I've slipped up. What these thickets grow
All wreathed with isn't ivy-creepers.
Come now, it's the barley-mow.
Best spread that plaid beneath us!

10

INDIAN SUMMER

The leaf of the currant is coarse in weave.
The house shouts laughter, glasses ring.
Indoors they salt, and pepper, and cleave up
And cloves are dealt out for preserving.

Derisively a wood pelts down
Its steep declivities all these sounds,
To where the burnt-up hazel stands
Consumed in sunlight, all a bonfire brown.

Here is a way down to the sunk place,
Here for old sticks that parch and shrink
And for ragman Autumn it's a hard case,
Sweeping everything down this sink;

Hard, that the world's way is shorter
And simpler than sharp ones pretend,
That the grove sinks down as in water
And each thing waits for its end;

That when all you are looking at goes
To ash, and the white soot of Autumn
Hauls gossamer over windows,
The look of it all is mindless.

A path breaks through a garden fence
And is lost among birches. There, indoors,
Laughter sounds, and the buzz of household
    chores.
That buzz and laughing also come from the
    distance.

11

WEDDING

Cutting over into the yard
The guests for the wedding-wake
Have moved in for the night at the bride's
    house,
Come with a concertina.

Behind the doors with felt on them
Of the man whose place it is,
From one in the morning till seven
There's not much noise of talking.

But as dawn comes up, in the depths of dream
When you're set to keep on sleeping,
The accordion cuts loose again
Lighting out from the wedding.

And he's spread it around, the accordionist
Making again with the squeeze-box
Spatter of clap-hands, bead-strings' glitter,
Whooping it up at a party.

And once more, once more, once again
The beat of the *chastushka*
Through to the sleepers together in bed
Has burst in out of the hubbub.

20

And there she goes, as white as snow
Riding it out, wolf-whistles, ting-a-ling,
Smooth into that peacock-step again,
Swung hips parading,

With a head to the beat rocked,
Right hand pulsing
In a peacock's stalk on the board-walk,
Peacock, a peacock dancing.

And the yard, the having fun,
The tread of the set-to-partners,
Are gone to hell out of it suddenly,
All washed up like water.

And it's come awake, the buzzing yard.
An echo of business deals
Has cut in on the talking
And the laughing spells.

Into the sky, unlimited, up
In an upswirl of dove-motes
Pigeons in a flock have spurted
Towering out of dove-cotes.

As if to be minded of these
In a wedding's wake were to stir
Well-wishings for many a year
Sent out to overtake them.

Life right enough is likewise only an instant
Only a loosening out
Of ourselves among all others
As it might be a thing we gave them

Only a wedding, blue deeps of a window
That it irrupts through upward,
Only a song that is sung, a dream,
Only a dove-blue pigeon.

12

AUTUMN

I gave up my people to go their several ways.
All that were near me long ago went asunder.
Now a loneliness I am used to
Fills all my heart and all the natural order.

And here I am with you, in an out-station
In a forest uninhabited and untrodden.
As it says in the song, the bridle-track
Is all to seek, the choked ride half-forgotten.

Now we are by ourselves, in a bad way,
And the walls of hewn logs scrutinize us blankly.
To take in our stride was never in the contract.
What we have to do is ride for our fall frankly.

We shall sit down at one in the morning, and at
    three
I shall let my book, and you your sewing, drop.
When day comes we shall not know
What made the kissing stop.

Ever more grandly, ever less guardedly, come
Into your clamours, uncover your seed-pods,
    leafage.
Let yesterday's cup, with its taste of sourness,
    brim
Over again with asperities of today.

22

Predispositions, latchings-on, allurements!
Let these be loose in alarums of September . . .
Install yourself in the lisping Autumn! Either
Forget yourself, or else fade out, dismember!

You disembarrass yourself of clothes
As the spinney disembarrasses
Itself of leaves, when you fall
Into my arms in your wrap with the silk tassels.

You are the windfall of the false step taken
When to live is nausea worse than illness causes;
But beauty is intrepid in the making;
And this it is that, each to the other, draws us.

13

FAIRY STORY

In days of old
Through a fabled land
Rode he amain
Over hill and hollow.

He sped to the fray.
On the dusty plain
Rose up afar
A dark wood in the way.

A keen pang
At the heart griped him:
'Ware of the well-water,
Draw the girth tighter.

23

Nothing list the rider
But made his steed to bound
And flew he amain
To the woody mound.

Turned he at the barrow,
Came into the dry fosse,
Passed he through the glade
And the mount he has crossed.

And strayed by the hollow dell
Come by the dark way
Found he the beasts' trace
And water of the well.

And deaf to the summons sent
No heed to ill bode,
Down to the brink he rode,
Gave to his horse to drink.

By the stream a cave's mouth,
Before the cave a ford.
As it were brimstone burning
Flamed in the opening.

Smoke billowed dun-red
His gaze baffled:
With a cry far sped
Sounded the forest.

Thereat upon the cleft
The horseman, ware,
Stepped soft-foot straightly
To whence the voice calling.

24

Saw then the horseman,
Tightened his lance-hold,
Head of the dragon,
Scales, and the tail coiled.

Ardent from maw spilt
Light showed plain
Three boughtes a damsel round
Wound he her spine.

Body of the serpent
As a whip's lash folds her,
His swayed the neck there
On hers the shoulder.

By that land's usage
Was paid in fee
To the monster of the wood
A captive comely.

Folk of the land
Huts that were theirs
Ransomed by rent paid
Thus to the serpent.

Serpent it was that bound
Hands fast, enwound her,
Took into throes of
The scapegoat the offering.

Looked in supplication
To high heaven the horseman.
Couched for altercation
Clasped he the lance then.

Sealed close the eye's lids.
Heights. And the cloud's climb.
Rivers. River-fords. Waters.
The years, the spans of time . . .

Rider, the helm brast,
Brought down in combat,
True steed with hoof-spurn
Tramples the serpent.

Charger next dragon's corse
Heaped on the sandbar,
In a swound the rider,
The damsel stounded.

Sheen of the noon's arch
Azure, dulcet.
What's she? A tsar's child?
Slip of earth? Earl's blood?

Abounding gladness
Flows now in tripled tears,
Now to a dead trance
Lie they in durance.

Charged to new hardihood
Now, and now listless,
Life in the spent blood,
Unstrung the sinews.

Beat still the hearts of them.
Dame first, then man
Strives against cumber,
Fails into slumber.

Sealed close the eye's lid.
Heights. And the cloud's climb.
Rivers. River-fords. Waters.
The years, the spans of time . . .

14

AUGUST

As good as its word, not to deceive,
The sun thrust through in the early morning
As a slant-wise stripe of a saffron colour
Athwart the sofa from between the curtains.

It overlaid with a hot ochre
The vicinity of woods, the village homesteads,
My bed, the pillow moistened,
And the reach of wall behind the bookshelf.

I have remembered what the reason is
That my pillow is damp a little:
The dream I had was that you saw me off,
One by one threading the woodland.

You went in a bunch, singly and in couples.
What day this was, was borne
Suddenly home to someone; sixth of August
Old style, and Our Lord's Transfiguration.

As a rule, this day, light without heat of burning
Issues out of Mount Tabor,
And Autumn, clear as a signal given,
Holds all eyes riveted.

And you were going through the penniless, paltry
Stark, shivering alder-brush
To the red-as-ginger grove that marked the
  graveyard
Burning up like a morsel of gingerbread.

The quietness of its tree-tops
Had the portentous heavens for neighbour,
And with the tongues of roosters
Distances held protracted colloquy.

In the grove, like a ministry surveyor,
Stood Death amidst the graveyard,
His eyes on the face of my mortality
Sizing me up for a grave-pit.

Remarked by all, calmly arose
A corporeal voice. From near at hand
Rang out the voice of the seer I was,
Intact and uncorrupted:

'Farewell the azure of Transfiguration
And the gold of Saviour's Day the second.
In my fateful hour let the bitter brew
Be allayed by a last ministration of woman.'

'Farewell years that went uncalendared!
Woman I part from, an abyss,
A world of indignities you have dared!
I am the acres you have fought across.'

'Farewell to the swept wing, sleek and planing;
Intentness in flight as the will travels;
Image of the world, a presence in language;
And Authorship; and the working wonders.'

15

WINTER NIGHT

The snow, the snow all over the earth
From end to end swirling.
And the candle burning on the table,
The candle burning.

As in a summer swarm the midges
Fly to the flame,
Flew the flakes from without
To the windowframe.

The snowstorm moulded on the pane
Arrows and rings.
And the candle burning on the table,
The candle burning.

On the illumined ceiling
The shadows massed
Of crossed hands, crossed legs,
Fates that crossed.

With a thud on the floor a pair
Of shoes fell down.
The wax from the nightlight wept
On to a gown.

And everything lost in a murk of snow
Greying, whitening.
And the candle burning on the table,
The candle burning.

On the candle a gust from the corner.
Temptation's lick
Of flame grew lifted arms,
Cross-like, angelic.

Snow all the month of February.
And intermittently
The candle burning on the table,
The candle burning.

16

THE BREACH

At the door he starts to doubt
If the house is his. Her going
Was nothing short of a rout.
Everywhere, signs of ruin.

All through the rooms, chaos.
Particulars escape him,
What with tears in his eyes
And his head aching.

In his head since morning an unaccountable
   noise.
He remembers, or is he dreaming?
And why should thoughts of the sea
Through his head be streaming?

When through rime on windows
No sight to be seen of Creation,
The corneredness of yearning is
Doubly like wastes of ocean.

She was as dear to him
In her every feature
As the sea is near to a coastline
In each wave breaking ashore.

As the inundation of reed-banks
By chopped seas after a storm,
Ebbed over the floor of his soul
Her features and her form.

From the years hard-driven, unthinkable
Ruses for getting by,
A wave of fate from the sea-floor washed
    her
Up to him, high and dry.

Amid snags past reckoning,
Perilous straits to be passed,
The one wave bore her, bore her
Home, and secured her fast.

And now here she has flitted,
Perhaps much to her sorrow.
The breach devours them both.
Emptiness eats in the marrow.

And the man looks all about him.
At the moment of her exit
She cleared the chest of drawers
Topsy-turvey of all that was in it.

He prowls around, in the darkness
He slams back all the scattered
Odds and ends into drawers
Along with the sample cut-out,

And finds a needle stuck
Still in a piece of sewing,
And it brings her all back, and his tears
Are suddenly, covertly flowing.

17

RENDEZVOUS

The road lies buried in snow,
The burdened gables bend.
I go out walking;
Behind the door you stand.

Alone, in an autumn outfit,
You struggle for self-command;
Hat and overshoes wanting;
Gulping snow from your hand.

The darkening distance muffles
The shapes of fence and tree.
Alone in the snow falling
At the corner you confront me.

Streams fill from your scarf the cuffs
Of the sleeves of your coat. The air
In flecks of dew, condensing,
Sparkles about your hair.

A lock of pale hair, lifted,
Lights face, and scarf at throat,
Brightens the moulded figure,
Lights up the shabby coat.

Snow is wet on the lashes;
Pain at your eyes looks out;
Your whole aspect in keeping,
All of a piece throughout.

As if, under my rib,
Antimony-tipped
There grooved an iron nib,
Scoring my heart to imprint you;

And there in those same features
Humility dwelt apart
For ever, and so no matter
The world's unpitying heart.

And so it appears twice over,
This whole wide night of snow;
And fixing frontiers between us
Is more than I can do.

Who are we, though, where sprung from,
When out of all those years
Hearsay remains, but of us two, nothing
Under the sun appears?

18

CHRISTMAS STAR

The winter held.
Blew the wind over the steppe.
In the burrow under the hill-slope
Cold for the child.

Snugly the breath of the ox lapped him.
Beasts of the steading crave
Standing room in the cave.
Hazing the crib warm currents of air wrapped him.

Shaking their sheepskins free of the trash and hay,
The loose bed-straw,
The blear-eyed shepherds saw
Midnight stretch out from the rock-ledge where they
    lay.

Far in a field of snow a graveyard was,
And hurdles, epitaphs,
Wagons snowed to the shafts,
And over the burial-ground a welkin full of stars.

But right at hand, though never heard tell till then,
More faltering than the glow
Out of a watchman's window,
Glimmered the star that fared for Bethlehem.

It flared like a rick, like a thing no more
The sky's, or God's, a fired stack,
Incendiary's work,
Like a farm on fire, and blaze on a threshing-floor.

34

It stood up like a stack, a glare
Of hay and straw on fire
Burning on the entire
World's frame unnerved at the new star in the air.

The glow upon it throve still ruddier.
Something was meant thereby.
Three scanners of the sky
Sped, summoned by such fires as never were.

Behind them were carried on camel-back gifts.
And asses in harness, some smaller than others, lifted
Neat delicate hooves, stepping down from among the
    cliffs.

And in a strange glamour of the coming era
Were stablished afar all later transpirings,
All the ages would think of, orbed stillnesses,
    cherished aspirings;
All that would be of museums and art-collections;
All misdemeanours of fairies, all wizardly transactions;
All of the bright world's fir-trees, all the dreams of
    youngsters.

All the quiver of candle-light, all festoons,
All the noble artifice of coloured crepe . . .
. . . All meanlier, all nippingly, blew the wind over
    the steppe . . .
. . . All the apples, all the gold balloons.

One part of the pond obscured among the alders,
Part could be noted well athwart the trammels
Of rookeries and the tree-tops, by sheep-herders.
From where they stood they made out asses, camels
Clearly along the verge of the pond meander.
—Go we with the rest, and worship we the marvel—
They told each other, shrugging wraps on shoulders.

Trudging the rough snow thawed them out in the end.
Across the sheeted snow-field, mica-bright,
Led round a hut the prints of naked feet.
About these prints, as to flame of a candle-end,
Padded and shifted sheep-dogs in the starlight.

The frosty night took shapes of faery-lore.
Someone out of the snow driven and mounded
Walked all the time invisibly with them banded.
The dogs plunged on, something they peered about for
Dogging the shepherd-boy, and ill hap apprehended.

By this same road, through the self-same parish,
Went some few angels where the throng most tended.
Invisibly fared they the way there, fleshless,
But where they had passed were steps imprinted.

Come to the rock, they thronged, a press of people.
Brightness came up. The stems could be seen of
    cedars.
—Who are you out there?—asked Mary.
—Of shepherds and legates of heaven our breed is,
For the lifting of lauds to you both are we come
    here.—
—Together you may not. Tarry there in the entry.—

In the murk of before-dawn, the grey as of ashes,
Trampled the drovers, the sheep-breeders,
Talkers wrangled with riders,
At the hollowed-out drinking-trough
Braying of camels, the kicking legs of asses.

Brightness came up. Dawn the last stars swept
Like grits of ashes clear of the sky-vault.
Only the Magi out of that countless rout
Did Mary receive through the rock-cleft.

He slept, all a shining, in a crib made oaken,
As the moon beams in on a trenched-out hollow.
For him was the office of fleeces taken
By lips of the ass and the ox's nostril.

They stood in the dusk of a shippon, in the shade
Whispering, summoning only the barest word.
Of a sudden, slightly, one in the darkness stirred,
A Magus moved left of the crib by someone's hand,
And the someone gazed in: from the doorstep straight
    at the Maid
Like a guest that calls, the Christmas star looked in.

19

DAYBREAK

You meant my entire destiny.
Then came the war, the break-down.
For a long, long time to me
No sight vouchsafed, no sign shown.

Over the many years, still
Your voice brings its warning sound.
All night I have read your will;
As if I had fainted and came round.

It comes upon me to feel
For the people whose morning comes
Alive in them, renewed. I'd shake piecemeal
And to their knees the lot of them.

And I run downstairs as though
For the first time ever my way
Lay by these streets under snow
And the derelict causeway.

They shrug awake, and lights come up,
A house-fug, drinking tea. And in the space
They take to get to the tram-stop,
Town looks a different place.

Snowgust over the gates knits up
Close mesh of the falling flakes; and geared
To keep to time, the cup
Is left half-full, the dish is left half-cleared.

I feel for them, the whole concourse,
As if I had been in their skin;
Myself I thaw as the snow thaws,
My brow lours like the morning.

In me are folk un-named, and trees,
Children, home-keeping kin.
I am won over by these;
This only is where I win.

20

THE MIRACLE

He fared from Bethany to Jerusalem,
Foreshadowings of affliction weighing on him.

Burrs of brushwood scorched on the steep bluffs'
    oven,
Over the hovel nearby no blown smoke stirred;
Hot breath of the air, and the reedbeds there
    unmoving,
And on the Dead Sea repose immovably anchored.

With sourness at heart that vied with the sour
    sea-water
He fared, while behind a few clouds raggedly
    followed,
Along the dust-choked road to some man's shelter,
Fared to the town, where some He instructed
    gathered.

And so far sank He, self-absorbed and brooding,
A wormwood smell came up as the field saddened.
All stilled. Alone He midway along was standing,
And the terrain stretched, sheeted in unfeeling.
All swam and merged: the balmy air and the barrens,
The lizards, the gushing springs, the waters running.

A fig-tree rising no great distance off,
Utterly bare of fruit, nothing but leaves and wood,
He said to it: 'Do you do me any good?
Is your stockstillness anything to be glad of?'

'I hunger and thirst, and you—you barrenly flower.
Encountering you is comfortless as granite.
What a trial you are, and how devoid of talent!
Stay as you are to the world's last hour.'

Throughout the tree ran the quake of condemnation,
As the levin-flash along a lightning-rod
Flashed on the fig-tree sudden incineration.

Had leaf and branch and root and stem been granted
One moment's freedom, then the laws of Nature
Had made all haste, and doom been intercepted.
But a miracle is a miracle, a miracle is God.
When we are all at odds it comes upon us
Instantaneous, and when least expected.

21

EARTH

The Muscovite's house in town
Spring tumbles upside-down.
The moth from the clothes-press fumbles
The milliner's summer creations,
Mink is stowed into hold-alls.

On the mezzanine storey's timbers
The pots are aromatic
With stock and wallflower. Chambers
Breathe spaces, dust remembers
A pollen smell in the attic.

And the street is in collusion
With the myopic window,
The river breeds confusion
Of white night and the sundown.

April along the ranges
Of the corridors divulges
What life the outdoors is leading.
She knows a thousand instances
Of mankind's dooms and dangers;
She chills, by chance exchanges
With the snow-thaw, darkling fences
Dwelling on these proceedings.

The one half-afire, half-fearful tension
Out there at large, and lapped about,
     domestic.
All round the very air is not itself.

40

All one the willow's grille of twigs,
And the white buds' distention,
On the window sill, at the crossroads,
In the street, and at the work-bench.

Then why does the distance weep in mist,
And the humus reek so sourly?
It is here you find me in earnest;
I am called on to interest spaces lest
Past city boundaries the oppressed
Earth left to itself be lonely.

My friends and I foregathering
For this in early Spring
Make evenings of farewells
And feasts out of making wills,
That the hidden rill of suffering
Warm what exists and chills.

22

THE BAD DAYS

When in the very last week
He entered Jerusalem,
Hosannahs pealed, and the people broke
Branches off, to attend him.

But the days closed in on him, tough.
Scornfully the brows knit.
No heart touched by love.
Epilogue here, an end to it.

Skies as heavy as lead
Settled between the blocks.
Proofs the Pharisees wanted;
They played him along, the foxes.

In the temple obscure forces
Had skid-row apprehend him;
And the same inflamed consensus
That rooted for him, damned him.

The crowd from that part of town
Gawped at the gateway,
Jostled, waiting for the show-down,
Surged forward, surged away.

And a whisper threaded the quarter,
Everywhere the tip-off ventured.
The run to Egypt came into his thought,
And his childhood, as if he dreamt it.

And he remembered the bad land,
The scarp there, and that mountain
Where having the world to command
Was what he was lured with by Satan.

And at Cana the wedding breakfast,
The miracle leaving the table guessing,
And the sea like dry land that he crossed
In the fog, step by step, to the vessel.

And the down-and-out bunch in a hut,
And the candle lit at the top
Of the cellar stairs, that went out
For fear, as the risen stood up . . .

23

MAGDALENE I

Hardly night falls when there my devil is,
What I owe to my past, a mortgage.
There they come, they suck the heart from
    my side,
The memories of foul things I did
When, slave to the idiosyncrasies
Of the male, crazy, in a sort of rage,
I had the street for orphanage.

There are still a few minutes to go,
Then the quiet comes, quiet of the tomb.
But first, before these come,
My life gone to the limit
Like an alabaster casket
I am breaking up before you.

Oh now where should I be,
Schoolmaster to me and Redeemer,
If at the table Eternity
Weren't the new one waiting to be
Netted in the game by me,
Night after night my customer?

Straighten this out—what does sin amount to,
Death, Hell, burning sulphur, when
Here I am, for all the world to see
Knit in with you, like a graft to the tree it's
    spliced in,
By my own miseries past the telling over?

Jesus, your feet locked fast
In my knees, I am learning to clasp
The quadrilateral shaft
Of a cross perhaps. I am raped
Of feeling as into my body
I hold you strained, and primed for the grave
    already.

24

MAGDALENE II

Folk set themselves to rights for a party.
Keeping clear of this lot,
I wash down with balm from a bucket
Your feet without spot.

I can't even find the sandals.
Crying, I can't see.
My hair's come down, hanks of it
Hanging over my eyes caul me.

I've grabbed your legs into my skirt,
I've sluiced them with tears, and there
I've the beads from my neck for a cord around
    them, Jesus.
I've smothered them in a burnous of hair.

I see what happens now, each item of it
As if you'd had the whole thing grind to a stop.
Just now I'm so good at predictions
I can see through things, I'm a sybil.

Tomorrow the screen comes down in the temple,
We shall be bunched together at one side
And the earth wobbles under our feet.
I reckon it's sorry for me.

The escort will form up again in column.
They'll make a start to the movement away of
    horses.
Like a waterspout in a cyclone, over our heads
The sky will be torn open, round that cross.

I'll hurl to the ground at the foot of the
    crucifixion.
I'll be out of my mind, I'll gnaw my lips.
You'd clasp too many, hands that on the cross's
Arms stretch out to the tips.

Who is it for in the world, so much bounty,
So much hurt, such a capacity?
Is there so much of being and life in the world?
So much of colony, of river-run and spinney?

But they'll wear by, three times sun-up to
    sundown,
And ram such vacancy that through
All that terrific intermission
It's Resurrection I'll be thriving to.

25

GETHSEMANE

With an indifferent flicker of distant stars
Was the turning in the road illumined.
The road went round about the Mount of
    Olives,
Beneath it flowed the Kedron.

The plot of grass sheared off halfway across.
The Milky Way went on from there.
The grey and silver of the olive trees
Drove themselves into distance, treading air.

In the end there was someone's garden or
    allotment.
Parting from the disciples at the wall
He said, 'My soul is sorrowful unto death':
'Tarry ye here, and watch with me' he said.

He abdicated there without contention,
As if from things that he had borrowed once,
From his Omnipotence and wonder-working,
And now he was a mortal, and like us.

The night's remoteness seemed a region now
Of the annihilated and the null.
Space through all the frame of things lay empty.
The garden alone was place for living in.

And gazing down those murky intervals,
Alleyways that went nowhere out of nowhere,
For the cup of this death to pass from him
In a sweat of blood he pleaded with the Father.

46

Easing by prayer these mortal slackenings,
He went out through the paling. On the ground
Lay the disciples, overborne and drowsing
On the road's verges, sprawling among tussocks.

He roused them then: 'You has the Lord
   appointed
To live my days, yet like the clay you crumble.
The hour of the Son of Man is come.
To the hands of sinners he betrays himself.'

No sooner said than bursting in from nowhere
Appears a rout of serfs and tinker rabble
With fire and sword and in the forefront Judas
With all the treacherous kissing in his lips.

Peter at the sword's point held them off.
He smote an ear from off the head of one
Only to hear: 'Resolve no feud with steel.
Man, put up your sword into its place.'

Could not a myriad of wingèd legions
Dispatched here by the Father reinforce me?
Then, with no hair of mine so much as touched,
Should all my foes with never a trace be
   scattered.'

'The book of life turns over to the page
Which is a dearer relique than them all.
Now must that which was written come to pass,
So be it, and fulfilment. And amen.'

'See how the times turn allegorical,
How they catch fire in very course of turning.
In the name of the terror of their potency
I seek the tomb in voluntary pains.'

'I seek the tomb and on the third day rise,
And as the rafts come floating down the river,
To me for judgment like a string of barges
The centuries shall drift up from the dark.'

THE COMMENTARY

Notes to 'Hamlet'

The best commentary on this poem is by Nils Åke Nilsson, his essay 'Life as Ecstasy and Sacrifice', in *Scando-Slavica* (Copenhagen) for 1959. In particular Nilsson shows how for the understanding of this poem, alone in the whole sequence, it is essential to go for clues elsewhere than just to the sixteen chapters of prose narrative which in *Doctor Zhivago* precede the seventeenth chapter given to the poems. The other document by Pasternak which has to be called upon is an essay he published just after the war, on his translations from Shakespeare. Here Pasternak defines his own understanding of Shakespeare's *Hamlet*:

From the moment that the ghost appears Hamlet denies himself in order to do the will of him who sent him. Hamlet is not a drama of a weak-willed character but of duty and self-abnegation. When it is discovered that appearances and reality are irreconcilable, that there is a gulf between them, it is of no moment that the reminder of the falseness of the world comes in a supernatural form, and that the Ghost calls for revenge. It is far more important that chance has so willed it that Hamlet is chosen as the judge of his own time and the servant of a more distant time. Hamlet is a play of the high destiny, the drama of a vocation.[1]

In view of the scriptural allusion in the 7th and 8th lines, which bind this first poem of Zhivago's sequence with the last, 'Gethsemane', even more

---

[1] *Soviet Literature* 1946: 9, p. 51. Quoted by Nilsson, loc. cit.

striking are some of Pasternak's comments on Hamlet's soliloquy, 'To be or not to be . . .':

These are the most heartfelt and frenzied lines ever written on the anguish of the unknown at the gates of death, in strength of feeling they rise to the bitterness of Gethsemane.

The prose narrative does, however, offer to throw light on this poem. In the 11th section of Chapter Fifteen we are given what purport to be notes by Zhivago, found among his papers:

. . . cities are the only source of inspiration for a truly modern, contemporary art.

The seemingly incongruous and arbitrary jumble of things and ideas in the work of the symbolists (Blok, Verhaeren, Whitman) is not a stylistic fancy. This new juxtaposition of impressions is taken directly from life.

Just as they hurry their succession of images through the lines of their poems, so the street in a busy town hurries past us with its crowds and its broughams and carriages at the end of the last century, or its trams, buses and electric trains at the beginning of ours.

Where, in such a life, is pastoral simplicity in art to come from? When it is attempted, its pseudo-artlessness is a literary fraud, not inspired by the countryside but taken from academic book-shelves. The living language of our time is urban . . .

. . . The incessant rumbling by day and night in the street outside our walls is as much connected with our thoughts as the opening bars of an overture with the curtain, as yet dark and secret, but already beginning to crimson in the glow of the footlights. The incessant, uninterrupted rustle and movement of the town outside our doors and windows is a huge, immeasurable overture to life for each of us. It is in these terms that I should like to write about the town.

And this section of the notes ends with a significant comment by the supposed narrator:

There are no such poems in what has been preserved of Zhivago's work. Perhaps 'Hamlet' belonged to such a series.

It must be said that without this explicit indication no one would have associated this section of the prose with the poem. Hence the contrivance strikes me as cumbrous, and not altogether fair. For the single image of the binoculars is not enough to make 'Hamlet' a poem of urban experience such as the prose envisages. The point of the prose passage seems to be, by the use of the same theatrical metaphor as in the poem, to establish that the 'echoes' of line 3 are those of the audience's movements and chatter dying down as the curtain rises. This puts the speaker of the poem, the actor, in the same physical relation to his fellow-citizens as the poet behind the walls of his city apartment.

Without this the speaker of the poem, who is established as an actor playing Hamlet, as Hamlet himself, and as Christ, would not have been established as himself a poet. As the actor is to Shakespeare, so Hamlet was to his father's ghost, so Christ was to his Father, so we are to that same Father or to destiny. Thus the voice, whose remote echo we have to hunt from to know our time or our times, is in the first place Shakespeare, in the second place King Hamlet's ghost, in the third place God the

Father, in the fourth place (if you are a Marxist, as in some sense Pasternak was) it is 'the logic of history'. But in the fifth place—so the crucial prose-passage informs us—it is the voice of his anonymous fellows coming through to the poet, who will express their times for them.

The last line is proverbial, and will carry a lot of weight. Nilsson for instance says admirably:

Both Hamlet and Christ were set tasks by their fathers. What, then, is the task of the poet? Has he come to save mankind or to set the time in joint again? The poem says nothing about this. The poet is certainly surrounded by falsehood just as Hamlet was, but nothing is said to intimate that his task and duty is to fight it. What the poem has to say about the poet's task one has to look for in the last line with its tone of contemplation and gravity: 'Living life is no easy matter.' Life is the poet's task.

And for Pasternak, who saw Shakespeare's *Hamlet* as 'the drama of a vocation', life is not a field of experience to be crossed, but the path of a destiny to be found and followed. His *Doctor Zhivago* is the story of such a finding and following.

Notes to 'March'

In Chapter Four (the 2nd section) Lara is installed in the studio of an absent artist:

. . . near Smolensky Market. The flat was at the top of an elderly-looking two-storey house. There were draymen living in the other part of it and a warehouse on the ground floor. The cobbled yard was always littered with spilt oats and hay. Pigeons strutted about cooing and fluttered up noisily to the level of Lara's window; sometimes a drove of rats swarmed down the stone gutter.

This town-scape is clearly the source of the rural imagery in the last stanza of 'March'. This is also the scene for Lara's and Pasha's wedding, and for 'Wedding', the poem which treats of this, where the pigeons reappear. I cannot see any other place in the prose narrative from which are derived, specifically, the images in this poem. But a passage of the prose which should surely be remembered in relation to 'March' is one of those quoted in the notes to 'Hamlet'—that excerpt given in the 11th section of Chapter Fifteen from notes supposedly found among Zhivago's papers, in which the latter derides 'pastoral simplicity in art', condemns its 'pseudo-artlessness' as 'a literary fraud', and declares that 'the living language of our time is urban'. This should suffice to instruct the reader of 'March' (as of that later nature-poem, 'The Earth', which significantly takes up the image of dung) to see more than the description, 'nature-poem', suggests. Certainly 'March' is no charming water-colour of natural scenes; and 'Hamlet', which precedes it, should have prepared us to see, for instance, behind the image of 'dung', the tragic and Christian paradox of the man who loses his life that he may save it.

Notes to 'In Holy Week'

F. D. Reeve (*Kenyon Review*, Winter 1960) observes that the third line 're-phrases and re-locates the meaning of a famous line by Lomonosov'.

I have taken pains to be faithful to rhyme; both in its placing and its quality, and to the fluctuating metrical shape of the stanzas, so as to bring over the very intricate and original structure in which a liquid and richly chiming melody, repeatedly disrupted by deliberate dissonance, is never wholly lost.

The source of this poem is in the first five sections of Chapter Ten, 'The Highway', which take us to the Siberian town of Krestovozdvizhensk, grouped round its monastery in territory held by Admiral Kolchak and the Whites. We are told (Section 2): 'It was Holy Week, the end of Lent; winter was almost over.' That is to say, it was the week before Easter Sunday. Most of the images that are to get into the poem are present here in the prose. For instance, lines 14 to 17, and 18 to 21, plainly derive from this paragraph:

At the seventh hour by the Church's reckoning and at one in the morning by the clock, a dark low sweet humming drifted from the deepest of the monastery bells, which hardly stirred. It mixed with the dark drizzle in the air. It drifted from the bell, sinking and dissolving in the air, as a clump of earth, torn from the river bank, sinks and dissolves in the water of the spring floods.

The order of the images is the same, though the prose makes a connection between the bell-ringing and the water undermining, whereas in the verse, very interestingly, the two images are simply juxtaposed. Again, lines 38 to 43 are clearer if one has noted from the 2nd section some of the topography of the town. The religious procession making the circuit of the precincts is 'almost in the street' (literally, 'along the edge of the sidewalk'), because the main road 'skirted the monastery grounds . . ., for the green-painted icon door of the monastery gave on to the main square'.

But here is a difficulty. For we are given no reason to think that Zhivago was ever in Krestovozdvizhensk, in Holy Week or at any other time; and, since he has at this point been captured by the Reds, whereas this town is held by the Whites, there is every reason to suppose that he was not. The difficulty is the greater when we find some parts of the poem deriving from the scenes as experienced by a person Zhivago never met, Galuzina, the grocer's wife, who in the 3rd section leaves the service when it has barely begun, and wanders through the streets in the early hours. Lines 10 to 13 for instance derive from this passage about Galuzina:

The stormy sadness of her thoughts oppressed her. Had she tried to think them all out aloud, one by one, she would not have had sufficient words or time enough till dawn. But out here, in the street, these comfortless reflections flew at her in clusters, and she could deal with all of them together, in the short while it took her to walk a few times from the monastery gate to the corner of the square and back.

And the two quatrains (ll. 22 to 25, and 26 to 29), with their strongly marked contrast between the forest trees and the town trees, may owe something to Galuzina's reflections, in the 4th section, on country as against town.

How can Zhivago know a time and a place of which he has no experience, and know them moreover through the mind of a woman he never met? The answer is given in one way by the 2nd section of Chapter Eleven, where Zhivago, in another Siberian town, happens across Tyagunova, a woman he had known in the train from Moscow three years before, who had escaped from the train with the boy-conscript Vassya Brykin. It turns out that Tyagunova is Galuzina's sister, and she tells Zhivago about Krestovozdvizhensk and about her sister's troubles there. We are surely meant to think that this sketchy information, together with the evocative and ecclesiastical name (Krestovozdvizhensk means 'town of the Exaltation of the Cross'), is enough to give Zhivago his poem.

And after all, how could we think otherwise? We do not suppose that Boris Pasternak, in order to enter into the feelings of a commonplace woman in a Siberian town in Holy Week, during the Civil War, had to have been there at just that time, or had to have known just such a woman. And Yury Zhivago is to be supposed at least as good a poet as Boris Pasternak, with imagination and human sympathies just as acute.

What is interesting is that Pasternak should pose the problem and make us work out the solution. (I cannot see that the 2nd section of Chapter Eleven has any other function than just to supply it.) Evidently it was important to him to establish in this way how much a poet like Zhivago can make out of only a couple of bare hints. And it was (we may suppose) even more important to establish that Zhivago, who has already in the poem 'Hamlet' made such sophisticated not to say blasphemous use of Christian references, and who is to treat them with even more sophistication in later poems of the sequence, is able at this point to sympathize with the traditional barely formulated Christianity of Old Russia. That Christianity, as Zhivago imagines it in someone like Galuzina, and indeed as he contrives to feel it himself, is full of feeling for fertility ritual. Nevertheless what the poem presents is an urbanized and vulgarized version of that ancient Christian-pagan compound; and this prevents the poem from dissolving into a nostalgia for the archaic and the rooted.

Notes to 'White Night'

I am in danger of reading too much into this poem, but it seems a case where it is better to read too much than too little.

Some translators have rendered 'far-off time' in the first line by 'a distant past', and then have gone so far as to change every present tense into past, to support this reading. But it is an unsatisfactory reading in any case; for the daughter of a landowner from the steppes of Kursk does not figure in Zhivago's past, at least as we know it from the prose narrative.

A time may be distant in the future no less than in the past. And this may seem much to the point in view of some excellent remarks by F. D. Reeve in *The Kenyon Review* for Winter 1960. For Reeve acutely sends us, for a gloss on this poem, not to any happening that is recorded from Zhivago's lifetime, but to an occasion twenty years after Zhivago is dead. This is recorded at the end of the Epilogue, in the very last paragraphs of the whole narrative:

On a quiet summer evening in Moscow, . . . Gordon and Dudorov were again together, sitting by a window high above the immense city spreading away into the dusk.

They were turning the pages of a book of Yury's writings which Yevgraf had compiled, a book they had read more than once and almost knew by heart. In the intervals of reading, they exchanged reflections and followed their own thoughts. It grew dark so that they could no longer make out the print and had to put on the light.

Moscow below them and reaching into the distance—Moscow, the author's native town and the half of all that had befallen him—now appeared to them, not as the place where all these things had happened, but as the heroine of a long tale of which that evening, book in hand, they were reaching the end.

Although the enlightenment and liberation which had been expected to come after the war had not come with victory, a presage of freedom was in the air throughout these post-war years, and it was their only historical meaning.

To the two ageing friends sitting by the window it seemed that this freedom of the spirit was there, that on that very evening the future had become almost tangible in the streets below, and that they had themselves entered that future and would, from now on, be part of it. They felt a peaceful joy for this holy city and for the whole land and for the survivors among those who had played a part in this story and for their children, and the silent music of happiness filled them and enveloped them and spread far and wide. And it seemed that the book in their hands knew what they were feeling and gave them its support and confirmation.

At first sight this brings us no nearer than Hayward's and Harari's reading, to identifying the daughter of the gentry from Kursk. On the other hand some other puzzling features of the poem make more sense if it is regarded as Zhivago's prevision of some such occasion as this, than if it is his recollection of some unrecorded incident from his past. In the fourth quatrain the line *Orobeloyu vernost'yu tainye*, which I translate as 'Confidences safeguarded with apprehension', seems to be a direct reference to the ever-present fear of informers under the Stalinist regime; that is to say, to the police-state which was re-imposed or continued unalleviated after 1945, thus disappointing the hopes of Gordon and Dudorov that victory would lead to 'enlightenment and liberation'. Only a little less certainly, in the 7th stanza the sinister colouring of the image of Night as a barefoot wanderer, with its reference to 'conversation overheard', seems to re-create the same police-state atmosphere, playing upon the same apprehensions.

The odd thing of course is that the prose insists how the conversation between Gordon and Dudorov takes place in Moscow, whereas the poem locates its conversation no less emphatically in Petersburg. But the very paragraph which insists on Moscow also identifies the young lady from Kursk. 'Moscow . . . now appeared to them, not as the place where all these things had happened, but as the heroine of a long tale of which that evening, book in hand, they were reaching the end.' By this insistence, right at the end of the story, on how completely Zhivago is a Muscovite, and how entirely his story is a Muscovite story, Pasternak goes out of his way to make us notice how the second city of Russia, Petersburg or Leningrad, plays no part at all and is the locale of not a single incident in the whole book. There could hardly be a clearer directive to the reader; when he turns a few pages and comes to a poem which insists on how it is a poem of Petersburg, what is he to think? Surely he is meant to realize that this is a poem not to be read literally. It is to be read allegorically or symbolically—in a way which permits the heroine of the poem to be, not any human young woman, but for instance Moscow or Muscovite Russia personified. The Muscovite moves in imagination away from Moscow (to Petersburg), so as to see Moscow, and his own allegiance to her, more truly because in perspective.

Before dismissing this interpretation as far-fetched, one must take into account the accumulated resonance, for the Russian literary imagination, of these two names, 'Moscow' and 'Petersburg'. The very title of the poem is resonant in this way, and prepares the reader to listen for the resonance in what follows it. 'White Night'—merely the phrase itself, in isolation, sets up echoes of Pushkin, of Gogol, of Dostoievsky, of Blok; and of other writers who have treated this meteorological phenomenon peculiar to the Neva estuary. so as to re-create—not just as a locality but as one powerful element in the Russian imagination and Russian destiny—Petersburg, the fabricated city of Peter the Great, created by forced labour and an imperious act of will. As every schoolboy learns, Peter, the great westernizer, created this city to be Russia's window on the west; created it by fiat, all at once, on the model of such western cities as Venice and Stockholm. To Zhivago the Muscovite, Petersburg is indeed a window; but he looks out of that window *eastwards*, to Moscow and the steppes beyond. Moscow is not Kursk, and it is a long way from the steppes; it is only when they are looked at from Petersburg that Moscow and Kursk and the steppes seem to hang together, standing for all that in Russian which is not western. Zhivago is writing very deliberately in the tradition of Pushkin, Dostoievsky and Blok, when he sets up organically dishevelled Moscow against inorganically symmetrical Petersburg; Christian Moscow against Petersburg of the rationalist Enlightenment; village Moscow against civic Petersburg; homely and earthy Moscow against the unnatural dream-like beauty of the Petersburg waterfront. 'Skyscraper' in the second quatrain carries, in Russian as in English, all the converging significances of the modern, the inorganically symmetrical, and the humanly presumptuous.[1] The girl from Kursk is Moscow and the Muscovite temper; addressed in Petersburg and from Petersburg, where she is an alien, she becomes Russia, or the soul of Russia, or that in Russia which is brought to the West, not borrowed from it.[2]

If the girl is not literally a girl but indigenous Russia personified, and if Petersburg in the poem is not literally a locality but rather a state of mind or (precisely) a viewpoint, are the nightingales literally nightingales, or the trees literally trees? Surely they are not. If the low-voiced conversation is taking place high up in a skyscraper, its echoes will not reach to any garden literally at the foot of the building, nor among any trees that literally stand there.

[1] Dr. Monica Partridge points out to me the perhaps significant oddity of the post-Revolutionary word for 'skyscraper' in conjunction with the pre-Revolutionary name, Petersburg.

[2] On the 'stylization' of Petersburg in this tradition of Russian writing, see Waclaw Lednicki, *Russia, Poland and the West* (1954), *passim*.

And in any case no trees burst into blossom in an instant, as they do in the poem, nor do trees uproot themselves and come crowding out into roads. These episodes at the end of the poem we must in any case read as hyperbole; they cease to be fanciful or whimsical, they become imaginative, only when we have taken the allegorical meaning of springtime and daybreak. For Gordon and Dudorov conversed at nightfall—'It grew dark so that they could no longer make out the print'; and in summer—'on a quiet summer evening in Moscow'. Why then do the talkers in the poem converse at daybreak, and in spring? Surely it is to endorse what the prose affirms—that 'a presage of freedom was in the air throughout those post-war years, and it was their only historical meaning'. The day which breaks is the day of 'enlightenment', the spring is the springtime of 'liberation'.

It is illuminating at this point to compare Blok's treatment of the Petersburg theme in his unfinished poem, 'Retribution'. Because of what we know about Pasternak's peculiarly close feeling for Blok (see the notes to 'Christmas Star'), it is not surprising if, out of all the great Russian writers who had treated of Petersburg before Pasternak, it is Blok's treatment which is nearest to Zhivago's. And at the end of the second chapter of 'Retribution' (a novel in verse), Blok asks the reader if, 'going out on a white night', he has not heard, or dreamed that he heard, a sound from the sea; and if has not seen, in dream or vision, a phantom fleet blockading the mouth of the Neva, with the figure of Peter the Great himself standing on a frigate's deck. But then, changing from those who thus dream to others who are awake, Blok speaks of those who watch through the night, who can see another fleet and another dawn, the Tsarist fleet returning humiliated, mutinous, and vengeful from defeat by the Japanese, and the bloody dawn of Revolution reddening already over Port Arthur and Tsushima, the scenes of those defeats. Zhivago's poem is about those who watch through another night, and addressed to others who thus watch; it assures them, as Blok's poem does, that the dawn is indeed coming—but the dawn in Zhivago's poem will not be bloody. I find it quite conceivable that Pasternak intended the reader to pick up these allusions to the poem by Blok.

It is not that we need imagine Zhivago's poem as set on some night still further in the future than that on which Gordon and Dudorov sit and talk. For on that selfsame evening the ageing friends of the dead Zhivago were carried into the future. It seemed to them 'that on that very evening the future had become almost tangible in the streets below, and that they had themselves entered that future and would, from now on, be part of it'. What brings this about in the poem is the singing of nightingales; what brings it about in the prose is the reading of Zhivago's book. In the poem it is the nightingales which give voice to the Russian hinterland; in the Epilogue that voice is the voice of a dead poet. For 'nightingale' we may read 'inspired poet' throughout—'inspired' because the nightingales' singing is called 'crazy' (as it might be, 'possessed'), but also because what Gordon and Dudorov read is 'a book of Yury's writings *which Yevgraf had compiled*'; and the figure of Yevgraf, as we know from considering other poems, stands for poetic inspiration conceived of as full sympathy with living tradition.

Thus 'White Night' is of all Zhivago's poems the one which answers most exactly to Pasternak's saying: 'all art describes its own birth . . .' The trees which crowd into the road to wave good-bye do so, not as some loosely-anchored whimsical hyperbole about 'Nature' or 'Young Love', but according to the strict logic of symbolist poetry. These trees exist in the poem and nowhere else; it is the poem which determines their coming and their going, their planting, blossoming and fruiting. Since they are trees-in-a-poem, they need not and cannot observe the natural laws which govern trees-outside-of-poems. They wave good-bye because their end has come; and their end has come because an end has come to the poem which was the only world they existed in. What is astonishing, about this poem as about others in Zhivago's sequence, is that this extreme and militant aestheticism behind the poem does not in the least prevent it from dealing with issues as concrete and momentous as the Stalinist regime, and with others as sweeping and (in the Russian perspective) as 'classic' as the dialogue between Petersburg and Moscow.

I have used the word 'allegorical'. But with this poem, as with others of the sequence, an allegorical reading breaks down just as a literal reading does, though not quite so soon. Gordon talks with Dudorov; but the dead poet talks with them both, out of the pages of his book which lies between them; and inside the book the poet talks with his Muse in the shape of a young lady from Kursk. The one-to-one

66

equivalences of allegory break down at the point where we ask which of these several dialogues is the dialogue in the poem. The poem is all of these dialogues at once, no one of them exclusively; for the poem *is* what it is 'about'. We have moved from the world of allegory to the world of symbolism, where the dialogue inside the book is indistinguishable from the dialogue of poet with reader. For the reader too is 'inside the book', in the sense that the book which Gordon and Dudorov read surely includes this poem, 'White Night'—a poem which is about Gordon's and Dudorov's reading of it. Thus when Zhivago in the third quatrain speaks of 'This which I tell you quietly', he is speaking to the young lady from Kursk who is his Muse, he is speaking also to Muscovite Russia behind her, he is speaking also to Gordon and Dudorov who read him, and he is speaking also to those other readers, ourselves. What is more, he speaks of himself as speaking ('All art describes its own birth'); not just the narration he speaks about, but the narration he speaks—that is, the whole poem—is addressed to us, to all of us at once. We are all of us inside this poem, so comprehensive as it is.

It is only by proving itself so comprehensive as this, by gradually engulfing into itself every inch of available reality even to the several identities of its readers, that the poem can justify the claims which it makes for itself. F. D. Reeve says finely, of *Doctor Zhivago* as a whole, 'Zhivago, who sets out to reform the world and to minister to it, gradually gives himself over to transforming it'. And in this poem the transformation is so complete that it ought to prove to Gordon and Dudorov, and to us, how right Zhivago was to make this choice; since the only sure pledge of enlightenment and liberty to come is the human capacity for transforming experience into poetry.

Notes to. 'Foul Ways in Springtime'

'Spring Floods', a title which some translators have given to this poem, is inaccurate but not altogether misleading if it recalls the springtime floods which Zhivago saw on his train-journey from Moscow. Certainly among the images which nourished the poem must be, for instance, these, which come from the time of that journey (the 19th section of Chapter Seven):

There was plenty of room for the water to play. It flung itself down the rocks, filled every pool to overflowing and spread. It roared and smoked and steamed in the forest. It streaked through the woods, sinking into the snow which hindered its movement; hissing on level ground or hurtling down and scattering into dusty spray. The earth was saturated. Ancient pine-trees, perched on dizzy heights, drank moisture almost from the clouds and it foamed and dried a rusty white at their roots like beer-foam on a moustache.

But that last brilliant and jovial image is quite out of key with the poem, where the tone is ominous throughout. And the ominousness is foreshadowed in a quite different passage, which supplies the images of riding and of the nightingale, to be compounded with the images of violently loosened waters. This is the account, in the 15th section of Chapter Nine, of how Zhivago, having attempted to break with Lara, rides out from Yuryatin to his family at Varykino ('a homestead deep in the Urals'):

As the sun went down, the forest was filled with cold and darkness. It smelled of damp leaves. Swarms of gnats hung in the air as still as floats, humming sadly on a constant, high-pitched note. They settled on his face and neck and he kept swatting them, his noisy slaps keeping time with the sounds of riding—the creaking of the saddle, the heavy thud of hooves on the squelching mud and the dry salvoes bursting from the horse's guts. In the distance, where the sun was refusing to go down, a nightingale began to sing.

'Wake up! Wake up!' it called entreatingly; it sounded almost like the summons on the eve of Easter Sunday: 'Awake, O my soul, why dost thou slumber'.

Whether Zhivago obeys this solemn injunction, or disobeys it, is left carefully unclear; for what it prompts him to is regret for having broken with Lara, a conviction that this was premature, and a determination to go back on it. In other words the image of Lara pursues him as, in the poem, he feels that the waters do; and in fact later poems in the sequence, which repeatedly associate Lara with images of water, will abundantly confirm Edmund Wilson's guess that Lara's name ('Larissa'—the sea) has allegorical significance.

Just as the poem concludes with a reference to the partisans, so this episode in Chapter Nine closes when Zhivago, still riding home, is confronted by three Red partisans on horseback who carry him off to serve with their forces in the forest.

But these are only some of the associations which

accumulate through the novel to enrich the meaning
of this poem. Earlier in Chapter Nine (the 8th section)
Zhivago has committed to his diary some observations
on the nightingale's song:

Once again I wondered at the difference between their
song and that of all other birds, at the wide gulf left
unbridged by nature between the others and the wealth
and singularity of theirs. Such variety and power and
resonance! Turgenev talks about it somewhere—that
whistling, as if the demon of the woods were playing his
flute. There were two phrases that stood out particularly.
One was a luxurious, greedily repetitive 'tiokh-tiokh-
tiokh'. At the sound of it, the thicket, all covered with
dew, shivered as though with pleasure. The other was
grave, imploring, an appeal or a warning: 'Wake up!
Wake up!'

This indicates one of the literary allusions in Zhivago's
poem; for Turgenev's wood-demon or wood-goblin
gets into the last stanza. But two more principal allusions
are identified in an earlier part of the same entry in the
diary:

Chapter 7 of *Eugene Onegin* describes the spring, Onegin's
house deserted in his absence, Lensky's grave by the
stream at the foot of the hill.

> The nightingale, spring's lover,
> Sings all night. The wild rose blooms.

Why 'lover'? Well, it's a natural thing to say, it's fitting.
'Lover' is right. And then, he needed it for the rhyme.—
Or was he really thinking of Nightingale the Robber, the
one in the ballad? 'Robber Nightingale, the son of
Odimantiy'.

> At his nightingale whistle,
> At his wild forest call,
> The grass is all a-tremble,
> The flowers shed their petals,
> The dark forest bows down to the ground,
> And all good people fall down dead.

In colloquial usage, a man with a fine voice is called 'a nightingale'. And in the folk-poems called *byliny* the legendary hero *Soloveirazboinik* ('Robber Nightingale') is able to knock down his opponents merely by whistling. This provides Zhivago with a sort of oxymoron, holding together the two potentialities, alternately baleful and beneficent, of the season of spring and of spring phenomena like loosened waters and nightingale's singing. Certainly the other allusion, to Pushkin, works in this way. For the lines which Zhivago quotes are from the 6th stanza of Chapter Seven of *Eugene Onegin*. In Babette Deutsch's translation:

> Within the hill-encircled valley
> Come seek the stream that slowly goes
> Through meadowland and linden alley,
> On down to where the river flows.
> The nightingale, this season's lover,
> There sings all night; wild roses cover
> The bank; one hears a gentle spring;
> And where two pines their shadows fling
> A gravestone tells its mournful story.
> The passer-by may read it clear:
> 'Vladimir Lensky slumbers here,
> Who early found both death and glory,
> In such a year, at such an age;
> Take rest, young poet, as thy wage.'

71

But more instructive are the 2nd and 3rd stanzas.

> Ah, spring, fair spring, the lovers' season,
> How sad I find you! How you flood
> My soul with dreams that challenge reason,
> And with strange languor fill my blood!
> My stricken heart cries out and fails me
> When once the breath of spring assails me,
> Although its touch be soft as fleece,
> While I lie lapped in rural peace!
> Is it that I was born to languish,
> And all that sparkles, triumphs, sings,
> Is alien to my breast, and brings
> No gift but weariness and anguish
> To one whose soul has perished, and
> Who sees the dark on every hand?
>
> Or is it that we fail to cherish
> The tender leaves, but in the spring
> Mourn those that autumn doomed to perish,
> The while we hear the woodland sing?
> Or are our thoughts in truth so cruel
> That nature's season of renewal
> But brings to mind our fading years
> That no hope of renewal cheers?
> Or it may be that we are taken
> In our poetic reverie
> Far back to a lost spring, and we,
> By dreams of a far country shaken,
> Recall with pain the vanished boon:
> A night of magic, and a moon . . .

Obviously T. S. Eliot in 'The Waste Land' was not the first to hear a voice saying:

> April is the cruellest month, breeding
> Lilacs out of the dead land, mixing

> Memory and desire, stirring
> Dull roots with spring rain . . .

And just as plainly Zhivago hears spring's nightingales 'fulminate', not out of any modish wish to reverse normal expectations, but from taking to heart the most classic poem in Russian literature.

He takes it to heart because it corroborates his own experience. For indeed, the cruel ambiguity of the spring is so nearly the central theme of the whole of *Doctor Zhivago* that in discussing it at all apart from the wealth of illustration which that work brings to it, we run the risk of dissolving it away into commonplaces and cloudy abstractions. We find ourselves saying that the season of life is by that token the season also of death—and this is an observation so portentously general that it engages with nothing in particular that we have experienced. Yet something like this is just about what the sum of Zhivago's experiences means to him; and the perception may regain some of its edge if we consider two in particular of Zhivago's experiences, which seem to point this way. One is the experience of writing poems, the other is the experience of assisting at a burial. The burial is that of Zhivago's mother-in-law, in the 17th section of Chapter Three:

That day the hard frost had broken. It was a still, heavy day, a day of ended frost and of departed life, a day meant for a funeral.

How far Pasternak is from resting inertly on stereotyped responses to the fact of spring may be seen from the ambiguity, here, of 'departed life': human life has indeed departed, but natural life has returned.

And the stock responses are to the fixity of frozen winter as apt for death, the setting in of the thaw as a symbol for life; Pasternak reverses the equations. And yet it is not just a case of arguing that black is white. For, ten sentences later:

Yura walked on alone, ahead of the others, stopping occasionally to let them catch up with him. In answer to the challenge of the desolation brought by death into the life of the small community whose members were slowly pacing after him, he was drawn, *as irresistibly as water funnelling downwards*, to dream, to think, to work out new forms, to create beauty. He realized, more vividly than ever before, that art has two constant, two unending preoccupations: it is always meditating upon death and it is always thereby creating life. He realized that this was true of all great and genuine art; it was true of that work of art which is called the Revelation of St. John, and of all those works which have been completing it throughout the ages.

I have ventured to italicize a phrase in this paragraph, to bring out how impossible it is, by the time we get to the poems, to take a reference to flowing water as simply descriptive, meaning no more than it says.

Moreover, 'nightingale' inevitably carries over to this poem the significance which accrued to it in 'White Night'. It is Zhivago's poetic destiny which calls him, at once promising and minatory, and appropriately in the accents of Pushkin, from the nightingale's throat. And before the poem is over Zhivago has answered the call and embraced the destiny. For he answers the question of the seventh quatrain— 'What paramour . . .?'—by realizing that the nightingale's challenge is addressed to him, Zhivago. The evidence is in the next quatrain, where the nightingale (identified by the allusion to Turgenev) comes from the bivouac of a wanted man, such as Zhivago then was, to confront a detachment of the partisans, just as Zhivago did at just this point in the story.

Notes to 'Explanation'

Dr. Johnson, who believed apparently that poetry is better the more translatable it is, says in his Life of Denham, of four verses from 'Cooper's Hill':

The lines are in themselves not perfect; for most of the words, thus artfully opposed, are to be understood simply on one side of the comparison, and metaphorically on the other; and if there be any language which does not express intellectual operations by material images, into that language they cannot be translated.

So we may say of this poem that, if there be any language in which the extreme and ecstasy of sexual desire is not expressed by the same word as serves for the extreme and ecstasy of passive suffering, into that language it cannot be translated. Fortunately English is not such a language; and the swing of meaning in English between 'passion' and 'Passion' reproduces almost exactly the ambiguity, crucial to this poem, in the Russian word *strast'*.

It is attractive, and perhaps it is correct, to see 'Explanation' as the one poem by Zhivago in which he does justice to the third woman in his life, the undemanding and shadowy Marina who is his companion in Moscow in the last years of his life. Certainly the first eight lines, with their reference to a specific Moscow building, the Manège, suggest this.

On the other hand these recall also Zhivago's bad dream after he has got back to Yuryatin from the partisans (Chapter Thirteen, the 8th section):

Now he dreamed of a dark winter morning; the lamps were lit and he was in some crowded Moscow street. Judging by the early morning traffic, the trams ringing their bells and the yellow pools of lamplight on the grey snow of the dawn-lit street, it was before the revolution. He dreamed of a big flat with many windows, all on the same side of the house, probably no higher than the third storey, with drawn curtains reaching to the floor.

Inside, people were lying about asleep in their clothes as in a railway carriage, and the rooms were untidy like a railway carriage, with half-eaten legs and wings of roast chicken and other remnants of picnic foods scattered about on greasy bits of newspaper. The shoes which the many friends, relations, callers and homeless people, all sheltering in the flat, had taken off for the night were standing in pairs on the floor. The hostess, Lara, in a dressing-gown tied hastily round her waist, moved swiftly and silently from room to room, hurrying about her duties, and Yury was following her, step by step, muttering dreary, irrelevant explanations and generally making a nuisance of himself. But she no longer had a moment to give him and took no notice of his mutterings except that she turned to him now and then with a tranquil, puzzled look or burst into her inimitable, candid, silvery laughter.—This was the only form of communication that remained between them. But how distant, cold and compellingly attractive was this woman to whom he had sacrificed all he had, whom he had preferred to everything, and in comparison with whom nothing had any value!

The time of day, and all the colouring and atmosphere of the scene, are quite different in the poem and in the dream; but the relationship between Lara and Zhivago in the dream is obviously in important respects identical with the relationship between the man and the woman in the poem. The different feel and colour of the scene seem to have been dredged up from farther back—from an incident on Yury's journey from Moscow to Yuryatin with his family. At one point on this journey, the passengers spend three days clearing the snow from the blocked railway-line, beside a village which has been burned down by Strelnikov's independent partisans. This is told in the 15th and 16th sections of Chapter Seven:

They became almost fond of the ruined station, as of a mountain shelter on a climbing holiday. Its shape, its site, the details of its damage remained in Yury's memory.

Every evening they returned to it when the sun—out of loyalty to old habits—set, just as it had always done, behind the birch outside the telegraphist's window.

A part of the outside wall had fallen in and cluttered up the room, but the window was still there and the corner opposite remained untouched, with its coffee-coloured wallpaper, the tiled stove with a round vent and a copper lid, and the inventory of the office furniture in a black frame. Exactly as before the disaster, the setting sun crept over the tiles and lit a warm brown glow on the paper and hung the shadow of the birch on a hook like a woman's scarf.

This episode seems to come into the narrative for the sole purpose of being recalled by the reader when he gets to this poem, with its grotesque fancy of the sunset nailed to the wall, which corresponds exactly to the shadow of the birch-tree hung on a hook. And for the same reason we are told that the details of the scene 'remained in Yury's memory'. It is the dream's curiously fugitive impression of a railway carriage which seems to have drawn up with it, into the brooding memory of the poet, this scene which he saw from a railway carriage which was a temporarily stationary home for 'friends, relations, . . . and homeless people'. These eight lines demonstrate as in a controlled experiment how the poetic imagination modifies the materials which memory presents to it —modifies them in a way that is like, and yet unlike, the ways of dream.

If Lara is in the poem as well as Marina, so is Tonya:

To Yura, his old friend Tonya, until then a part of his life which had always been taken for granted and had never needed explaining, had suddenly become the most inaccessible and complicated being he could imagine. She had become a woman. By a stretch of imagination he could picture himself as an emperor, a hero, a prophet, a conqueror, but not as a woman.

Now that Tonya had taken this supreme and most difficult task on her slender fragile shoulders (she now seemed to him slender and fragile, though she was a perfectly healthy girl), he was filled with that ardent sympathy and shy wonder which are the beginning of passion.

With this passage, from the 10th section of Chapter Three, Zhivago's wife, first in order of time among the women in his life, is seen to be comprised along with others in the generic figure of Woman which the poem celebrates.

But it is Lara, as might be expected, who is present

most insistently. The image from electricity in the 7th quatrain recalls Zhivago speaking to Lara at Varykino (Chapter Fourteen, the 3rd section, italics mine):

When you—a shadow in a schoolgirl's dress—arose out of the shadows of that room, I—a boy, ignorant of you—with all the torment of the strength of my response, at once understood: *this scraggy little girl was charged, as with electrical waves, with all the femininity in the world.* Had I touched you at that moment with so much as the tip of my finger, a spark would have lit up the room and either killed me on the spot or filled me for the rest of my life with a magnetic flow of plaintive longing and sorrow. I was full to the brim with tears, I wept and blazed inwardly. I was mortally sorry for myself, a boy, and still more sorry for you, a girl. The whole of my astonished self asked: if such is the torment of being charged with the energy of love, *what must be the torment of being a woman, of being this energy, of being its source?*

And ten pages later, in the 9th section of this chapter, 'In the rush of some task or other their hands would meet and join and then they set down whatever they were carrying weak and giddy, all thoughts driven from their heads.'

However, if there is more than one woman in the poem, so also there is more than one man. Astonishingly, many of the verses might be spoken not by Lara's lover, Zhivago, but by her despicable seducer, Komarovsky. In particular the penultimate stanza, dwelling on one item after another of a woman's anatomy, is the litany of a sensualist. It recalls nothing so much as Komarovsky's realization, in the 13th section of Chapter Two, that he has committed himself far more deeply than he intended, to the schoolgirl he has seduced:

> What he needed desperately was Lara and there was no possible chance of seeing her that Sunday. He paced up and down the room frantically, like a caged animal.
> She had for him the unique charm of the incorporeal. Her hands astonished him like a sublime idea. Her shadow on the wall of the hotel room had seemed to him the outline of innocence. Her vest was stretched over her breast, as firmly and simply as linen on an embroidery frame.
> His fingers drummed on the window pane in time to the unhurried thud of horses' hooves on the asphalted carriage-way below. 'Lara,' he whispered, shutting his eyes. He had a vision of her head resting on his arm; her eyes were closed, she was asleep, unconscious that he watched her sleeplessly for hours on end. Her dark hair was scattered and its beauty stung his eyes like smoke and ate into his heart.

But how could Zhivago know what had gone on in Komarovsky's heart and head? It is the same question that we ask about the unintelligent woman who experienced the poem 'In Holy Week', and it must get the same answer: it is part of what the poetic imagination means, thus for the poet to be able to sink his identity in the identity of another. This is what Zhivago says himself at the end of 'The Wedding' and again at the end of 'Daybreak', just as Keats had said it before him. But in any case, where Komarovsky is concerned, we have other evidence of Zhivago's clairvoyance, in the conversation he has with Lara in the 12th section of Chapter Thirteen, where he confesses his jealousy of Komarovsky and justifies it in a way to which Lara has no answer.

It is indeed one of the strengths of Pasternak's treatment of love in *Doctor Zhivago*, as of Zhivago's treatment of it in this poem, that it is unflinchingly erotic.[1] There is no question of distinguishing sharply between a 'pure' love (Zhivago's) and an 'impure' (Komarovsky's). On the contrary one of the things that goes wrong with Lara's marriage to Antipov is that Antipov's love for her is altogether too 'pure' to be sustaining. The image from electricity is not used lightly; what is released in sexual encounter is *energy*, creativity as such—hence the reference to '*spring*'s fever-fit'. And this is as true if the sexual partner is Komarovsky as if it is Zhivago. Even Komarovsky, at the start of Chapter Four, feels after his fashion 'the passion for the break'—'in no circumstances must he come near her; on the contrary he must keep away . . .' And while I agree with F. D. Reeve (*The Kenyon Review* for Winter 1960) that part of what is pointed to in the last quatrain of 'Explanation' is the necessity for the artist of abnegation and self-induced suffering, yet it would narrow the poem further than I like, to suppose that the passion for the break is known in love only by artists.

It is probably unnecessary to point out that, none the less, in the poem woman is not seen and celebrated solely in her erotic capacity. The very touching 3rd and 4th quatrains are there to celebrate woman's doggedness and selfless fidelity, so that the celebration in the poem widens to include, for instance, the

---

[1] Accordingly perhaps the oddest of all comments on *Doctor Zhivago* is Renato Poggioli's reference to Zhivago's '*almost fleshless* love for Lara' (my italics). See Renato Poggioli, *The Poets of Russia 1890–1930* (Harvard, 1960), p. 333

wives of the partisans in the *tayga*, and an indomitably resourceful family of spinster sisters in Yuryatin.

When all is said, however, we cannot allow the presence in this poem of women in all their human-ness to shut out the sense that the being whom the poet addresses is as much 'Russia' as she is 'Woman'. Renato Poggioli, speaking of statements which could be cited from Pasternak's verse, early and late, remarks:

all of them sound like apologies which the poet addressed not so much to the régime as to public opinion, or rather, to an élite able to understand equally the reason of poetry and the reason of state. Yet the poet seemed to know, at least in the depth of his heart, that any reconciliation between art and politics was fundamentally impossible. Hence that sense of both pride and shame in all of Paster-nak's statements on the subject: the pride of his uncon-querable loneliness, and the shame of being unable to pay the Revolution the tribute which all pay, and which may well be justly due to it.[1]

The mixture of shame and sullen pride in the tone taken by the speaker of 'Explanation' answers exactly to Renato Poggioli's description. It is what gives to the poem its memorable and peculiar flavour. And it follows that this is one of the places where Zhivago and his creator are most at one.

Notes to 'Summer in the City'

In the original this poem, like the others in quatrains, rhymes *abab*.

This poem is a very interesting case indeed; at

[1] Renato Poggioli, op. cit., pp. 335–6.

least I have found it so. For a long time it seemed to
me that the point it made was not sufficiently sharp.
I found myself wanting the word 'unfading' in the
last line to be 'unflowering'; in this way, I conceived, the reference to lime-trees would make explicit
what the earlier stanzas would have implied—the
sterility of the relationship between the man and
woman, implied also in the growling thunder. But
this would have been a stratagem too sophisticated
and oblique for the limpid surface of late Pasternak;
and on re-reading the prose narrative I realized how
impossible it was for the scent of lime-trees, associated as it constantly is with the flowering at Melyuzeyevo of love between Zhivago and Lara, to stand
in any way for sterility in human relations. Very late
in the day I found what I believe to be the point of
the poem, and a very sharp one it is.

Briefly, as I now think, the poem presents a night
spent by Zhivago and his wife Tonya, on which breaks
in the last stanza, along with the daylight, Zhivago's
guilty awareness of how Lara has alienated his
affections.

This reading depends upon identifying the
thundery night quite specifically as one of which
we are told in the 4th section of Chapter Six, a night
on which Tonya throws a party to celebrate her
husband's return from the Western Front. As the
guests are leaving—

It thundered once as if a plough had been dragged right
across the sky. Then silence. Then four loud, delayed
thuds, like overgrown potatoes being flung out of the
soft, newly dug beds in autumn.

The thunder cleared a space in the dusty, smoke-filled

room. All at once, like electrical currents, the component elements of life became perceptible: air and water, need for joy, earth, sky.

The side street filled with the voices of the departing guests. They had started an argument of some sort in the house and were still arguing in exactly the same way in the street. Gradually the voices became softer in the distance and at last faded away.

'How late it is,' said Yury. 'Let's go to bed. The only people I love in the world are you and Father.'

We know at this point in the novel that this profession of Yury's, however sincerely he wishes it to be true, in fact is false. We know it because of what, in the prose and the verse alike, is associated with the fragrance of lime-trees. At Melyuzeyevo, the hospital where Zhivago had got to know Lara was 'the former residence of Countess Zhabrinskaya' (the 4th section of Chapter Five). Loitering on his way to an awkward interview with Lara still known to him only as Nurse Antipova, Zhivago had looked out of a window of the rambling house (section 6):

And from the Countess's centuries-old garden, so littered with fallen branches that it was impenetrable, the dusty aromatic smell of old lime-trees coming into blossom drifted in a huge wave as tall as a house.

When, next night, Zhivago gets his interview with Lara, before he shocks them both by stumbling into an implicit avowal of his love for her, Lara is ironing:

The windows were open. In the room the scent of lime blossom mixed, as in an old park, with the caraway-bitter smell of dry twigs; to it were added the charcoal

84

fumes of the two flat-irons which Lara used alternately, putting them each in turn in the flue to keep them hot.

And the lime-scent follows Zhivago to Moscow. In the train which takes him there from Melyuzeyevo he continues to smell it (section 13):

Then, like a message delivered on the way or like greetings from Melyuzeyevo, as though addressed personally to Yury, there drifted in the familiar aromatic smell. It came from somewhere to one side of the window and higher than the level of either garden or wild flowers, and it quietly asserted its excellence over all else. Kept from the windows by the crowd, Yury could not see the trees; but he imagined them growing somewhere very near and spreading over the carriage roofs their tranquil branches covered with dusty leaves as thick as night and sprinkled with constellations of small, glittering wax flowers.

Everywhere along the way there was the noisy crowd, and everywhere the lime-trees were in blossom.

Their scent seemed to be everywhere at once and to overtake the travellers on their journey north, like a rumour flying round each siding, signal-box and half-way halt and waiting for them on arrival, established and confirmed.

Obviously, when the fact of lime-trees is dwelt upon with such wealth of attention, we do wrong if we read them merely as shorthand for the heroine. They are made very fully present in their own right, as products of Russian earth; and indeed the point of associating them with Lara is not to enrich them but to enrich her. By force of this association she comes to typify and embody the Russian earth in her own person.

And thus there is a deeper resonance to the poem. For the loving lie which Zhivago tells Tonya after the party is only the last of many which he has told that evening as, tipsily, he has joined in with the half-baked pro-Revolutionary enthusiasm of his guests. When in the prose 'the component elements of life become perceptible', they challenged and discredited this also; and in the same way the unfading lime-trees of the poem stand for Lara, but also for more than Lara.

Notes to 'Wind'

In the 16th section of the Conclusion, Lara says to Zhivago's corpse, 'Your going, that's the end of me.' This poem is as it were Zhivago's anticipating this response and answering it.

As in other poems of this sequence, the wind here surely has the symbolic meaning it had for Blok, and for Pasternak in his 'Four Fragments about Blok'.

Notes to 'Barley-mow'

The original turns on a punning double-meaning to the word 'Khmel', which means in the first place 'hops', and also, more generally, 'intoxication'. A similar ambiguity in the English expression, 'barley-mow', appeared the nearest equivalent. The translation is thus, inevitably, 'free'.

Notes to 'Indian Summer'

Several images in this poem recall the opening sections of Chapter Twelve, 'Iced Rowanberries', which have to do with how autumn comes to the partisan encampments in the Siberian *tayga*. Certainly 'the white soot of Autumn' in the 5th stanza seems a very interesting and effective conflation of two images in the prose of Chapter Twelve, the 5th section:

The weather was horrible. A sharp, scudding wind swept torn clouds, as black as flying soot, low over the earth. Snow fell from them in insane white flurries . . .

The connection is worth making, if only to emphasize how essential this poem is to the sequence, since among so many others of 'nature-worship' here is one which emphasizes rather the mindlessness of nature, and how its processes seem discredited by contrast with the prudent foresight of the human activities of housekeeping. From this point of view, 'derisively' in the 5th line is important; the wood is imagined as scornfully jeering at human precautions against a wintriness which takes nature and the wood unawares. The laugh is turned upon the foolish wood, before the poem is through.

All the same the contrast between human thrift and natural fecklessness is reconciled in the last line of the poem. For it would be banal for Zhivago to mean, by the laughter and commotion from a distance which answer to their likes indoors, only that in other houses the same activities are going on. The sense is, surely, that despite appearances something in the natural order answers to this in the human; the mushrooms, as it were, are asking to be pickled.

For the form the housekeeping takes is of the first importance. As George Katkov observes of the first line, 'The black-currant leaf . . . would suggest to a Russian the season of pickling and salting cucumbers and mushrooms. Black-currant leaf was used widely as a herb for making brines.' And thus, more than Zhivago's memories of the *tayga*, what informs the poem are his memories of Varykino—and of his first stay there, with his wife Tonya, rather than his second, with Lara. For, as Katkov says, 'the theme of this poem is the daily round of domestic life seen to proceed in harmony with the changes of the seasons'. To be sure, the harmony is discovered only at the very end, and most of the poem is concerned with establishing, rather, a dissonance. In the diary which Zhivago keeps at Varykino (the first sections of Chapter Nine), he explicitly warns us: 'I am not preaching a Tolstoyan doctrine of simplicity and "back to the land".' Yet the same diary records sentiments which are certainly implicit in the poem; for instance, 'What happiness it is to work from dawn to dusk for your family and yourself, to build a roof over their heads, to till the soil to feed them . . .' Even more to the point is another entry in the diary, in the 2nd section of Chapter Nine:

We have been lucky. The autumn was dry and warm. It gave us time to dig up the potatoes before the rains and the cold weather. Not counting those we gave back to Mikulitsin, we had twenty sacks. We put them in the biggest bin in the cellar and covered them with old blankets and hay. We also put down two barrels of salted cucumbers and two of sauerkraut prepared by Tonya. Fresh cabbages hang in pairs from the timbers . . .

For here, along with the pickling and preserving which lead into 'Indian Summer', is a reference to the cellar where the preserved vegetables are stored. And the cellar, as it is described and dwelt upon a few sentences later, figures with startling effect in the last lines of 'The Bad Days', a poem near the end of the sequence. Accordingly 'The Bad Days', which has as much to do with Christ and the raising of Lazarus as with Zhivago in his cellar, is intended, as I conceive, to recall 'Indian Summer' and to draw tangibility and concreteness from that connection.

As important as Zhivago's memories of Varykino, and far more important than the *tayga*, are what gets into this poem from Zhivago's experiences on his long trek back to Moscow from the Urals. The woods running 'in deep gullies to the river, dropping precipitously'; the unnaturally intense burnt colours of the 2nd stanza ('so ominously rusty brown, the colour of old, dimmed gold') and above all the hazel-tree—these come from the powerfully written 2nd section of Chapter Fifteen, where Zhivago, 'at the end of the summer and the beginning of a warm, dry autumn', moves slowly through a landscape devastated and largely depopulated by the Civil War, And this makes it certain that what is intended in the last lines of the poem is the Rilkean conception of how inanimate nature yearns for the human to perfect it and preserve it. In Rilke the inanimate asks to be preserved in human utterance, in the names man finds for it; though this idea is entertained by Zhivago also (for instance at the end of 'Earth'), in 'Indian Summer' and elsewhere Nature asks rather to be cropped, so that it may renew itself in a new season. In Chapter Fifteen, for instance, it is rye that is 'ominously rusty brown', and Zhivago notes, of 'these flame-coloured fields burning without fire, these fields silently proclaiming their distress', that 'usually when it is cut on time, its colour [the rye's, that is] is much lighter'. The case appears the same with the hazel:

Usually the nuts are not allowed to ripen, as people, and particularly village children, pick them green, breaking off whole branches. But now the autumn-wooded hills and gullies were thick with rough golden leaves dusted and coarsened by the sun, and festive among them, as if tied with ribbons, were bulging clusters of nuts, three or four together, ripe and ready to fall out of their husks.

But the festive simile reinforces a point explicitly made—that these fruits of the woods differ from fruits of the fields. Zhivago fed on hazel nuts for a week, and no doubt gratefully; but 'he felt as if he saw the fields in the fever of a dangerous illness'.

Notes to 'The Wedding'

This poem presents the translator with special and probably insurmountable difficulties. It is in the metre of the *chastushka*, a form of popular composition which is mentioned explicitly in the 5th quatrain. Traditionally a peasant dance tune, the *chastushka*, according to George Katkov, is now to be thought of as a 'popular ribald factory song', usually to the accordion. I have no way of being sure about the level and tone of the poem's diction but at some points, as one might expect of language set to this metre, it appears to be racy and colloquially vulgar. See for instance the 8th quatrain, where in place of Hayward's and Harari's (and Kamen's) very stilted reference to Tartarus, I have risked, 'Gone to hell out of it.' This illustrates how, in order to get into current English any vulgar energy and verve, one has to draw upon American rather than British speech—because British youth in fact uses American idiom for such purposes. But even American idiom provides only poor and approximate equivalents.

Apart from the difficulties presented by the language the topography of the poem is hard to understand, as are the social and human relations which it takes for granted. The time-sequence is clear enough, though translation can disastrously obscure it. But what is the relation of the yard to the house where the bride sleeps? And to neighbouring houses? Is the yard a public place, or private, or semi-private? And if it is to some degree private, what is its relation to the public thoroughfare?

Similarly, as regards the man of the house, explicitly mentioned in the 5th line, what is his relation to the bride? Is he the bride's father, and therefore host to the wedding guests? Or is he on the contrary only the resident householder? Or even just a neighbour?

These questions can be settled only by reference to the prose narrative, which thus contributes to this poem in an unusual way—not primarily as a source of images (though it is that too, as we shall see), but as a source of indispensable factual information.

The wedding appears to be that of Lara and Pasha Antipov, recounted in the 3rd section of Chapter Four. (The 4th section, which deals with a second party nine days after the wedding party, is also drawn upon.) Lara has no father. Indeed she lodges alone; and both the wedding party and the farewell party which succeeds it take place at her lodgings. These have been described at the end of the 2nd section of Chapter Four; they consist of a studio-apartment belonging to a painter who is away in Turkestan—

. . . Lara moved to the lodgings Kologrivov had recommended, near the Smolensky Market. The flat was at the top of an elderly-looking two-storey house. There were draymen living in the other part of it and a warehouse on the ground floor. The cobbled yard was always littered with spilt oats and hay. Pigeons strutted about cooing and fluttered up noisily to the level of Lara's window; sometimes a swarm of rats swarmed down the stone gutter.

Given this information, I find it certain that the felted door behind which we are taken in the 2nd quatrain is that of 'the draymen' who share the house with Lara, who accordingly figure as 'the householder' only in the sense of being senior co-tenants. And the yard, it now seems, is neither wholly private property nor wholly public; the yard of a warehouse abutting on the street whence one may hear quite naturally, as in the 9th quatrain, 'an echo of business deals', as customers come in the morning to argue the price of corn and straw. (As already noted, this is also the yard of the last quatrain of the poem, 'March'.)

If the 2nd quatrain takes the reader into the draymen's quarters, does he ever emerge again? I think in one sense he does not. For they share the first floor with Lara, and it is to their window that in the last quatrain the sound of the wedding floats up (from the yard, not, as Hayward and Harari say, 'from the street'), just as the pigeons fly up to and past Lara's window on the same level. A doubt which remains is whether the draymen are the sleepers in the 5th quatrain. I think they may be, but since 'bed' is in the singular, and also because it will be very odd if there is no reference at all to the marriage-bed, I have risked suggesting that the sleepers here are bride and bridegroom tired out after love-making.

And after all we should not be surprised if the poem takes us floating in and out of consciousnesses which are normally distinct. For this experience and the importance of it, is explicitly evoked in the penultimate stanza:

> Life right enough is likewise only an instant
> Only a loosening out
> Of ourselves among all others
> As it might be a thing we gave them.

In the very instant of saying this we float, along with Zhivago, into another consciousness altogether—that of the Jewish boy, Misha Gordon, many years before (the 7th section of Chapter One), on a long train-journey:

All the movements in the world, taken separately, were sober and deliberate but, taken together, they were all happily drunk with the general flow of life which united and carried them. People worked and struggled, they were driven on by their individual cares and anxieties, but these springs of action would have run down and jammed the mechanism if they had not been kept in check by an over-all feeling of profound unconcern. This feeling came from the comforting awareness of the interwovenness of all human lives, the sense of their flowing into one another, the happy assurance that all that happened in the world took place not only on the earth which buried the dead but also on some other level known to some as the Kingdom of God, to others as history and yet to others by some other name.

It is effective and profound to have this perception proffered to us by those anonymous Russians, the draymen. (Misha, incidentally and significantly, can perceive but not experience this 'profound unconcern' and 'awareness of the interwovenness'; this limitation he sees as part of what it means to be a Jew—at least in Russia.) The value to be put on anonymity—this comes best from those who are anonymous, wholly tangential to the narrative.

This quality of the tangential, and the poignancy of it, are at the heart of the poem. Who is it, for instance, who goes dancing like a peacock? She is a nameless apparition conjured up, like everything else (for this is a poem in which nothing is *seen*), out of the sounds which drift upwards and penetrate the sleeping consciousness of Lara and Pasha perhaps, but more importantly of those complete strangers who sleep next door to them. The peacock-dancer is thus the embodiment of all that is poignantly transitory and fugitive; yet it is worth having Lara hear the sounds also, since this brings home a particularly sharp instance of transience—the way in which on only one day of her life is a woman a bride (and a brilliant peacock), a single day earned by the many more on which she is to be a wife (a domesticated pigeon). The dancer is thus not the particular bride, Lara, but *the idea* of a bride.

As in all the poems, so in this one it is essential to remember that it is the artistic composition of one man, Zhivago. We must suppose that the salient details of the wedding party and the farewell party were supplied to Zhivago by Lara, out of musing recollections. (These would have included, I think, an image from the prose which does not get into the poem though it somehow stands behind it, in our experience of prose and poetry together—the hobbled horse which strays into the yard during the night.[1]) The fluctuating and merging of consciousness is made plausible to us by the way the sounds penetrate the sleepiness of those who hear them. But in fact the one consciousness which can comprehend all the others, entering into the minds of the draymen and of Lara and even of a Jewish schoolboy, is the consciousness of the poet. And so it is relevant to remember, in relation to the penultimate stanza, Keats's remarks on how the poet lacks 'character':

A Poet is the most unpoetical of any thing in existence; because he has no Identity—he is continually in for—and

---

[1] Chapter Four, the 4th section—'A hobbled horse was moving across the yard with short limping jumps. She did not know whose it was or how it had strayed into the yard. The sleeping city seemed dead. It was bathed in the grey-blue coolness of the early hours. Lara closed her eyes, carried to goodness knows what country depths and joys by the noise of the horse's hobbled steps, so unlike any other sound.'

filling some other Body—The Sun, the Moon, the Sea and Men and Women who are creatures of impulse are poetical and have about them an unchangeable attribute —the poet has none; no identity—he is certainly the most unpoetical of all God's Creatures . . . It is a wretched thing to confess; but it is a very fact that not one word I ever utter can be taken for granted as an opinion growing out of my identical nature—how can it, when I have no nature? When I am in a room with People if I ever am free from speculating on creations of my own brain, then not myself goes home to myself; but the identity of every one in the room begins so to press upon me that I am in a very little time an(ni)hilated . . .[1]

It is in keeping with the sustained drive of *Doctor Zhivago* towards apotheosis of the poet, that what Keats sees as a peculiarity in some ways disabling, Pasternak offers as an ideal norm of feeling.

Notes to 'Autumn'

If George Katkov is right when he sends us, for the source of this poem, to nothing in *Doctor Zhivago* but rather to 'Chapter from a Novel', a document published in the thirties, 'Autumn' is a poem as to which the pretence that it was written by Yury Zhivago breaks down completely.

This is surely a view to be resisted as long as possible, for if it is accepted it invalidates what I have taken to be the idea and governing principle of the whole sequence. And so it is a relief to find that much of the poem can be traced quite con-

[1] *The Letters of John Keats*, ed. M. B. Forman, 3rd ed., p. 228 : letter dated 27th October 1818.

fidently to certain pages of the novel, specifically to passages about how Zhivago returns with Lara to Varykino, where he had earlier been settled with Tonya and his children. In the 3rd section of Chapter Fourteen, when Lara proposes retreating from Yuryatin to Varykino, Zhivago responds:

But about Varykino. Of course, to go to that wilderness in winter, without food, without strength or hope—it's utter madness. But why not, my love! Let's be mad, if there is nothing except madness left to us.

This is exactly the mood conjured up in the poem. And it is elaborated in the prose, beautifully and to the point:

But after all it's true, isn't it, that we haven't any choice. Put it how you like, but death is really knocking at our door. Our days are really numbered. So at least let us take advantage of them in our own way. Let us use them up saying goodbye to life, let us be alone together for the last time before we are parted. We'll say goodbye to everything we held dear, to the way we looked at things, to the way we dreamed of living and to what our conscience taught us, and to our hopes and to each other. We'll speak to one another once again the secret words we speak at night, great and peaceful like the name of the eastern ocean . . .

When in the 4th section of Chapter Fourteen Yury and Lara, with Katya, make their retreat to Varykino, the effect of hysteria in the whole venture is sustained in Zhivago's deliberately madcap driving of the sleigh. It is significant however that the move, as well as the debate about it, happens at midwinter; and the autumnal imagery must therefore be drawn from another chapter of Zhivago's life, perhaps from the autumn which he experienced with the partisans in the *tayga*.

An attractive but ultimately unacceptable reading of the poem is offered by F. D. Reeve, writing in *The Kenyon Review* for Winter 1960. Reeve writes, of the last stanza:

Zhivago cannot endure the continued immediacy of so much life, the pressure of so much undefined insistence. The world being what it is, and not Lara's world, he can preserve her vitality only by fraud and by art. He can keep her only by sending her away and by transforming into the ordered language of poetry, as a definition, his sense of the electricity that passed between them.

It is good to find a reader for whom it matters that Zhivago is a poet. And undoubtedly the paradoxes of aestheticism are not foreign to Zhivago's experience, any more than to Pasternak's. Moreover this comment makes as good a guess as any at two very riddling passages—one in the verse (the last stanza of 'Explanation'), and one in the prose, Zhivago's tricking of Lara into going with Komarovsky to the Pacific sea-board,[1] a perverse step which it is possible, but not very plausible or interesting, to attribute to straightforward altruism. On the other hand, as a gloss on this poem in itself, Reeve's comment is surely top-heavy: it depends on taking 'beauty' ('krasota'), in the penultimate line, as strictly the beauty of art; and the context gives no warrant for reading this common and powerful word so narrowly.

[1] Accordingly there may be significance in the punning play, in the passage last quoted from the novel, on the word 'pacific'.

Notes to 'Fairy Story'

In the 9th section of Chapter Fourteen Zhivago feels that the wolves round Varykino represent the hostility which will drive him and Lara from that retreat —an intangible hostility which 'loomed like a prehistoric beast or dragon . . . who thirsted for Yury's blood and lusted after Lara'. And there are other hints in this section of the prose narrative by which Pasternak seems to invite us explicitly to explore the background to this poem by considering the place in the Russian tradition of the legend of St. George and the Dragon. Edmund Wilson followed this signpost in his valuable essay, 'Legend and Symbol in "Dr Zhivago"',[1] and so did George Katkov in his notes to translations by Henry Kamen.[2] Mr. Katkov's observations are particularly welcome, since they have to do, not just with the substance of the poem, but with its style:

The story of St. George, as it spread through the oral tradition of the 'Religious poems' (*dukhovnye stikhi*), sung by the Russian equivalent of minstrels, is a fusion of the Byzantine story of the martyrdom of St. George and the western version of the liberation of the 'maiden' from the dragon. This explains the mixed style of imagery, in which the Russian landscape combines with a somewhat westernized medieval style.

In my version I have tried to reproduce this 'mixed' and 'westernized' style, by drawing on the diction of

[1] *Encounter*, 69 (June 1959).
[2] Pasternak. *In the Interlude—Poems 1945–1960*, tr. by Henry Kamen (1962), pp. 123–4.

Spenser's *Faerie Queene* which itself is modelled in part on that of the English mediaeval romances.

A supplementary 'source' for the poem may be found in Chapter Seven. 'The Journey' (the 24th section):

The white northern night was ending. Everything was clearly visible, the mountain, the thicket and the ravine, but as if they did not quite believe in themselves and existed only in a fairytale . . .

The waterfall, though not far away, could be seen only from the edge of the ravine beyond the thicket. Vassya Brykin, the escaped conscript, had tired himself out with joy and terror looking at it.

There was nothing comparable to the waterfall anywhere in the neighbourhood. It was unique and this made it terrible, transformed it into a being endowed with life and consciousness, perhaps that of the dragon or winged serpent of these parts, who levied tribute and preyed upon the countryside . . .

The references here to fairytale and dragon lead into the poem as directly as those which come along with St. George. A few sentences later we learn that Vassya Brykin has been hiding by the waterfall for two days, after his escape from the troop-train bound for the Eastern Front ('He sped to the fray'), and that he is accompanied by the woman Tyagunova, a virago whom we have met as the mistress of an older conscript. (For Vassya is no more than a boy.) What Vassya says to her reveals, or hints, that at the time of the escape Tyagunova had tried to murder her rival Ogryskova.

This gives point to stanza 13, in which the physical confusion between woman and serpent seems conveyed with grotesque insistence in the Russian. (It is incidentally all-important, surely, to preserve meticulously Zhivago's switching from 'dragon' to 'serpent' and back again.) At this point in the poem the woman in the serpent's toils cannot help but recall the figure of Eve the temptress. And indeed the Freudian imagery seems to be consistently sustained, so that the whole can be read as an allegory of sexual encounter.

But what is more important is to realize that the woman in the poem, if she is Tyagunova, is also Lara, when seduced for instance by her mother's protector Komarovsky (hence 'ransom' and 'scapegoat'), just as she is also the Mary Magdalene of later poems in the series. In fact this poem should prevent us from sentimentalizing Lara, the heroine. Seen through Zhivago's eyes she is profoundly ambiguous, a force as much destructive as creative. And of course in the plot Lara does in many important ways destroy Zhivago her lover, just as she destroyed her husband, Pasha Antipov, by transforming him into the Gerald-Crich-like figure of the avenging man of will, Strelnikov. (I refer to D. H. Lawrence's *Women in Love*.) Moreover Lara is identified with a waterfall when Zhivago dreams, in the 8th section of Chapter Thirteen, of maltreating his son by Tonya, the child Sasha whom he has abandoned for Lara's sake.

It is important to realize that 'Fairy Story' is presented, like the rest, as Zhivago's poem, not Pasternak's. At first it may seem that this cannot be, because Zhivago, in the train from which Brykin has escaped, has no way of knowing what has happened to Brykin. But I think we should take the poem, and also the corresponding section of the prose, not as the omniscient narrator's account of what happened to Brykin, but as Zhivago's imagining of what might have happened, or (better) what, according to the logic of the poetic imagination, *should* have happened.

Indeed, it is only on this understanding that, for instance, the 17th section of Chapter Seven can be seen to provide anything more than anecdotal local colour; for in this section nothing happens except that Zhivago and his wife overhear Ogryskova and Tyagunova quarrelling about who shall have Brykin. It was essential that Zhivago should have this information in order that the image of predatory temptress woman should come together with the waterfall he hears later in the journey (in the 21st section), so as to make his poem for him. There could not be a better example of how the novel cannot be appreciated—the necessity of its component parts cannot be recognized—until prose narrative and poems are considered as making up one thing. To put it another way, the escaped conscript is connected with the waterfall, not because the waterfall was near where he escaped (it is not certain that it was), but because we are told about the waterfall, or about some one waterfall, that 'Its freshness *and freedom* widened the expanse of the night and it was this that had filled Yury with happiness in his sleep' (the 21st section of Chapter Seven—my italics).

In Chapter Fourteen (the 9th section), we are given Zhivago's experience when writing this poem:

He started with a broad, spacious pentameter, but its harmony, derived from the metre itself and independent of the sense, annoyed him by its slick, humdrum sing-song. He gave up the pompous rhythm and the caesura and cut down the lines to four beats, as you cut out useless words in prose. The task was now more difficult but more attractive. The writing was livelier but still too verbose. He forced himself to still shorter lines. Now the words were crammed in their tetrameters [*sic*] and Yury felt wide awake, roused, excited; the right words to fill the lines came, prompted by the measure. Things hardly named assumed form by suggestion. He heard the horse's hooves riding on the surface of the poem as you hear the trotting of a horse in one of Chopin's Ballades. St. George was galloping over the boundless spaces of the steppe. He could watch him growing smaller in the distance. He wrote in a feverish hurry, scarcely able to keep up with the words as they poured out, always to the point and of themselves tumbling into place.

There is something wrong here, since, if the lines were shortened 'to four beats', *and then shortened again*, it can hardly be tetrameters that the words were 'crammed in'. And in fact this is a mistranslation: the word is 'trimeter'. Sure enough, no line in the poem is longer than a trimeter, and most are shorter still.

We should note that there is a real distinction between 'harmony derived from the metre itself and independent of the sense', and 'the right words . . . came, prompted by the measure'. For prompting is not dictation. And in another excerpt from the diary (6th section of Chapter Nine), Zhivago exclaims, thinking of Pushkin: 'What a lot depends on the choice of metre!'

Notes to 'August'

Henry Gifford has helped me generously by answering my queries about this poem. From him I learn, for instance, as regards the puzzling second line of the third stanza from the end, that the Orthodox Church observes in early August three days called respectively the First, the Second, and the Third Saviour; August 6th (O.S.) is the second of these.

The stately resonance of these lines, dignified by Church Slavonic, should not lead us to read into the poem more levels of meaning than one. The 'gold' of this day, for instance, has been established insistently through 'saffron' and 'ochre' and 'red-as-ginger'; the colouring is literal, not (except very marginally indeed) ritualistic or symbolic. And in the same way 'the azure of Transfiguration' boldly registers the other component in the landscape as physically observed—the blue of the skies which, in the seventh stanza, are neighbour to the tree-tops.

Double-meaning appears only in the last stanza, and in fact in the last line; where there is a sort of pun in the words translated as 'authorship and 'working wonders'. The wonders can be miracles. And the authorship can be, as it is in English hymns of the eighteenth century, the originating activity of God the Creator. The poem thus leads up to an apotheosis of the artist, who in his art both transfigures the world and can be transfigured himself. And of course the poet is resurrected posthumously in his poems.

Notes to 'Winter Night'

At the end of stanza 4, Obolensky's 'crossed destinies' (*Penguin Book of Russian Verse*) is very beguiling. But it invokes a little too loudly the 'star-crossed lovers', Romeo and Juliet. And this invokes for Zhivago and Lara a stock response from the reader which makes the rest of the poem superfluous.

In the penultimate stanza to write 'wings', as Obolensky does, seems foolish. For the Russian word can mean 'arms' as well as 'wings'; and an angel has arms as well as wings, but a cross has only arms. Moreover the gesture is surely one of benediction. In the 3rd section of Chapter Fourteen Zhivago says to Lara, 'It's not for nothing that you stand at the end of my life, my secret, forbidden angel, under the skies of war and turmoil, you who arose at its beginning under the peaceful skies of child-hood.'

What the poem recalls very insistently is Lara, in Chapter Fourteen (the 8th section), waking and sleepily whispering to Zhivago, 'Still at work, my love? . . . Burning and shining like a candle in the night.' And most readers, surely, will associate the poem with Lara's and Zhivago's tormented idyll at Varykino (Chapter Fourteen), though they will read erotic meanings into the image of discarded clothing, and so will want the candle to stand for Zhivago's love-making as well as for his working through the night at his poems. Indeed no one will deny that the subject here *is* erotic. And as Obolensky points out, the rendering of it with such chasteness is what we are prepared for in the 14th section of Chapter

Fourteen, where we learn how hard Zhivago works at his poems:

The reason for this correcting and rewriting was his search for strength and exactness of expression, but it also corresponded to the promptings of an inward reticence which forbade him to expose his personal experiences and the real events in his past with too much freedom, lest he should offend or wound those who had directly taken part in them.

And yet in the 8th section of Chapter Fourteen we have been told that this poem, together with 'Christmas Star', had been composed before the return to Varykino though only there was it committed to paper. It appears therefore that it cannot treat of Zhivago's life there with Lara. And in fact there are strong indications that the episode it is meant to recall chiefly is from much earlier in Zhivago's and Lara's story, Lara's conversation with Pasha Antipov in the 9th section of Chapter Three, 'Christmas Party at the Sventitskys''. This took place in the same room in which, at the end, Zhivago lies in his coffin. And Lara grieving over the corpse, makes the connection:

She strained her memory to reconstruct that Christmas conversation with Pasha, but she could remember nothing except the candle burning on the windowsill and melting a round patch in the icy crust on the glass.

How could she know that Yury, whose dead body was lying on the table, had seen the candle as he was driving past, and noticed it, and that from the moment of his seeing its light ('The candle burned on the table, the candle burned'), all that was pre-ordained for him had seized control of his life?

What is quoted in parenthesis here is the refrain to Zhivago's poem, which I have rendered, 'And the candle burning on the table, The candle burning'. When Lara at Varykino alludes to the same lines, we may suppose that she is quoting back to the author his own poem, which he has recited to her at some earlier stage. And thus the poem may refer to the Varykino idyll after all. Indeed, it's essential that it should. For Lara's quoting of his own poem back at Zhivago is only one of many indications that by this stage in their story both Zhivago and Lara see each thing that happens to them as prefigured and pre-ordained; that they see themselves, in fact, as already characters in a story or at least in a developing drama. 'Hamlet', the first poem in the sequence, struck this note from the beginning and should have prepared us to listen for it later, as here.

As for the word 'candle', whenever it occurs in the narrative at any point after this episode, it has a symbolic resonance. However, this is symbolism at its most irreducible, at its furthest from allegory; for it is the very wealth of association that accrues to the word which prevents it from ever bearing a single formulable meaning. By the 16th section of Chapter Fourteen, for instance, the most common-place exchange about having enough candles, and whether they are of wax or tallow, bristles with symbolic overtones just because the speakers are Lara's lovers Zhivago and Antipov/Strelnikov.

Note. G. Katkov (*In the Interlude*, tr. by H. Kamen, p. 234) finds the reference to February in the last stanza an odd one, since in the prose the reference to a *Christmas* party is so

Notes to 'The Breach'

This poem, and 'Rendezvous' which follows it immediately, are obviously companion-pieces, products of the same experience, two beams of light falling at different angles on the one disturbance. One passage of the prose, in the 13th and 14th sections of Chapter Fourteen, tells of the composition of both poems. But 'The Breach' presents the experience nakedly and harshly, with all the jangle of jarred nerves; in 'Rendezvous' the trouble is distanced and more under control, though not for that reason less harrowing. Hence much of 'The Breach' can be glossed from the prose almost word for word, as 'Rendezvous' cannot:

He came in, locked the door behind him and took off his coat. When he came into the bedroom which Lara had tidied up so well and so carefully that morning, and which her hurried packing had again turned inside out, when he saw the untidy bed and the things thrown about in disorder on the chairs and the floor, he knelt down like a child, leaned his breast against the hard edge of the bedstead, buried his head in the bedclothes and wept freely and bitterly as children do. But not for long. Soon he got up, hastily dried his face, looked round him with tired, absent-minded surprise, got out the bottle of vodka Komarovsky had left, drew the cork, poured half a glassful, added water and snow, and with a relish almost equal

emphatic. He speculates that 'by letting Zhivago postpone the completion of the poem to a much later date Pasternak wanted . . . to give him an opportunity to relate the seemingly trivial episodes of his life to the great historical events that served as a background to it. The February in the poem might well be the February of 1917; . . .' I find this far-fetched.

in strength to the hopelessness of the tears he had shed, drank long, greedy gulps.

It is worth reading through to the end of the paragraph. When the narrative switches to the vodka-bottle, this is not to cover up with a gruff masculinity the supposed mawkishness of weeping. The clues are plain enough in 'absent-minded surprise'. Such abrupt veerings of attention are typical of a mind mastered by experience it cannot come to terms with. And this is the state of mind in the poem also: it merely breaks off, it does not reach a conclusion—if it ends with a burst of tears, they are not the sort of which one says, 'If only he could weep, he would feel better.' He has wept before, as the second stanza tells us; and no doubt he will weep again. (It goes without saying that we should not imagine Zhivago writing the poem in this stage; doubtless he recollects and re-enacts it much later—the poem is a controlled dramatizing of an out-of-control condition.)

It is because the state of agitated bewilderment has been established, that the questions in the third stanza are seen to be real ones. (In fact, rhetorical questions are quite foreign to Zhivago's way of writing.) The stanzas which follow, each an attempt to answer his own question why he should think of the sea—these are the meat of the poem. And if referring back to the prose should lead us to locate the poem in the first three stanzas and the last four, considering the sea-images that come between as just a decorative amplification of this discursive material, it would be better not to turn to the prose at all.

Some of the marine analogies are twisted, they cut more ways than one; this is why they can express mental agitation more faithfully than discursive statement could. No one of them reproduces the relatively straightforward analogy established in the prose (the 13th section of Chapter Fourteen), as Zhivago silently addresses the vanished Lara:

This is how I'll trace your image. I'll trace it on paper as the sea, after a fearful storm has churned it up to its foundations, leaves the traces of the strongest, furthest-reaching wave on the shore. Seaweed, shells, pumice, all the lightest debris, all those things of least weight which it could lift from its bed, are cast up in a broken line on the sand. This line endlessly stretching into the distance is the tide's high-water mark. This is how you were cast up in my life, my love, my pride, this is how I'll write of you.

What comes nearest to this is the 6th stanza:

> As the inundation of reed-banks
> By chopped seas after a storm,
> Ebbed over the floor of his soul
> Her features and her form.

(The sea here appears to be an inland sea, like the Caspian.) The relationships in this simile between man and woman, memory and separation on the one hand, reed-banks, chopped seas, sea-floor and storm on the other, are manifold and complicated, even mutually contradictory, beyond any teasing out in explication. What seems certain is that they give no warrant for comfortable assurance like Henry Kamen's:

> So all her features drown in him:
> Their hidden image he will keep.

On the contrary, this is one place where this poem and 'Rendezvous' seem especially closely connected.

110

The latter poem claims to hold an image of Lara which is indeed secure and inviolable. But this became possible only after the generalizing and universalizing which supervened, as we learn in the 14th section of Chapter Fourteen, on Zhivago's writing about the lost Lara. An image which ebbs on the sea-floor, that floor being reed-banks which stand clear of the water except in certain special conditions—this image is a very different matter, altogether more fluctuating and uncertainly agitated.

There is another sense in which the marine comparisons are at the heart of this poem. This sense is secondary because it has to do with 'The Breach' less as a poem than as a cryptogram or message in code. Just for this reason it is likely to excite commentators much more, if only because it can be illustrated at great length. To be brief, however, 'The Breach' seems to be the poem which gathers together more insistently than any other the punning significance of Lara's name, first pointed out by Edmund Wilson. 'Lara' is short for 'Larissa', which in the Orthodox calendar means 'sea-gull'; a pre-Christian mythological Larissa was wife to the sea-god Poseidon.[1]

One may be forgiven for suspecting at the start that this is a discovery of ingenious commentators, rather than anything truly in the written work. But the pointers are too many, and underlined too heavily; there can be no doubt that Pasternak

[1] Edmund Wilson is prepared to see also a more specific reference to the Trotskyite heroine Larisa Reisner (1895–1926), to whom Pasternak in 1926 devoted a poem 'In Memoriam Reisner'.

intended the pun. Of many passages that might be cited, one is particularly striking. It comes from Chapter Five, which otherwise is seldom drawn upon for the poems. At Melyuzeyevo, to which Zhivago is moved with his military hospital as the Western Front breaks up around him, Lara is serving as a nurse. Soon after she leaves to find her way home, on a night of storm a knocking at the door suggests to Zhivago and the oddly marooned little Frenchwoman, Mademoiselle Fleury, that Lara, balked of her intention, has returned and is seeking refuge.

Mademoiselle came back. 'Well?' said Yury. 'You were right. There's no one.' She had been all round the house; a branch knocking on the pantry window had broken one of the panes and there were huge puddles on the floor, and the same thing in what used to be Lara's room—there was a sea, positively a sea, an ocean . . .

They had been sure that, when they opened the door, Lara would come in, chilled through and soaked to the skin, . . . and would tell them her adventures, pushing back her hair and laughing.

They had been so sure of it that when they locked the door the imprint of their certainty remained in the street, round the corner, like the watery wraith of this woman, or of her image which continued to haunt them.

It is the cumulative effect of passages such as this, interspersed with others where the marine reference is more cursory and natural, which makes it indisputable that either a running comparison of Lara with the sea was intended throughout, or else (what Edmund Wilson does not allow for) that an experience such as this at Melyuzeyevo naturally though quite illogically makes the connection habitual with Zhivago.

George Katkov reports: 'Pasternak told his friends that the poem was a description of his own feelings when he learned of the first arrest of Ivinskaya in 1948.' This is very interesting, and no doubt true. But we can see that there is quite enough in the recorded experience of Yury Zhivago, to sustain the fiction that 'The Breach' is his poem rather than Boris Pasternak's.

Notes to 'Rendezvous'

This poem was published, with others of the sequence, in *Znamya* (Moscow) in April 1954. This first version, published in advance of the novel, lacked what is now the last stanza. George Katkov, who points this out, finds the last quatrain 'mysterious', and explains it by saying, 'Like other poems in the cycle, Meeting [i.e. Rendezvous] has a closer relation to Pasternak's own real life than to the events of the novel.' But is this really so? Is the last stanza so mysterious if we regard it as the work of Zhivago rather than Pasternak? Undoubtedly Katkov is right to say, 'The meeting is an imaginary one; the poet is meeting an image which is engraved . . . in his heart.' But this was an experience of the poet Zhivago, no less than (doubtless) of the poet Pasternak. Chapter Fourteen says as much. In its 13th section, after Zhivago has tricked Lara into leaving him, he soliloquizes:

I'll stay with you a little, my unforgettable delight, for as long as my arms and my hands and my lips remember

113

you. I'll weep for you so that my lament will be lasting and worthy of you. I'll write your memory into an image of infinite pain and grief. I'll stay here till this is done, then I too will go. . . .

In so far as this 'lament' can be located in any one poem, rather than in the sequence as a whole, it may surely be located here. If so, we should look in this poem for 'an image of infinite pain and grief'. And it is at this point that the distinction between Pasternak and Zhivago turns out to be, as usual, something more than a quibble. For Katkov, treating the poem as immediately Pasternak's, reads the last stanza so as to make the poem end, as it were, on an up-beat. For him, the revelation that the meeting was imaginary means that the union of the lovers is inviolable : 'It is this humble vision which makes the union of the lovers possible in spite of the "mercilessness of the world" which has separated them, and this accounts for the mysterious last strophe . . .' But surely F. D. Reeve does better (in *The Kenyon Review* for Winter 1960), when he sees the question posed in the last quatrain as not rhetorical but real, something not to be answered until the poems about the Magdalen at the end of the sequence. For him the stanza 'asks what man is for: how does he make an adequate definition of himself?' Whereas for Katkov the question in the last stanza sends us back to the arrogant affirmation of the 8th, for Reeve it opens up a whole dimension beyond that. And this seems to me preferable for several reasons: in the first place, so far as I understand Pasternak's view of poetry as essentially musical, this tends to produce poems which move always forward and end a long way from where they began, poems which are open-ended rather than neatly turned back upon themselves; in the second place, as I have hinted already, Reeve's reading makes the poem indeed a lament, full of pain and grief; and thirdly one should surely be chary of taking from Pasternak what seems to be a peculiarly Russian virtue, the capacity for asking massively direct Tolstoyan questions like, 'What is life for?'

Moreover, to take this poem on Katkov's terms leaves Pasternak wide open to an objection which is made to *Doctor Zhivago* by readers who are otherwise sympathetic:[1] that Pasternak too readily and too sweepingly writes off as incurably corrupt the whole world of political action and social organization. Only a mealy-mouthed humanitarian would object to 'No matter the world's unpitying heart' at the point where this comes in the poem; it is a lyrical cry of defiance from the personal fastness to which the world's ferocity has driven the speaker. But if this were to be the statement made by the poem as a whole (which is what Katkov's reading amounts to), one might legitimately object that it was inadequate and inhuman in the poet to regard the woes of the world as solved merely because he can retreat from them into an inviolable privacy. To regard the stanzas which follow as opening up dimensions beyond that act of private defiance—this is to see the writer acknowledging the inadequacy of that attitude, or at least recognizing the price that has to be paid for it.

A poem is necessarily a public document, as soon

[1] See, for instance, John Strachey, *The Strangled Cry*.

as it is published. And so, however closely this poem may correspond to passages in Pasternak's private life, it must be flawed as a poem unless it corresponds also to realities which are public and available. Those realities are experiences common to all mankind, ultimately; but in this sequence of poems there stands, between the private life of the poet and the life common to his readers, the life of the exemplary and representative man, Zhivago. And his imaginary interview with the lost Lara seems to be what we are told of, in an important passage of Chapter Fourteen. This is in the 14th section of that chapter:

He drank vodka and he wrote about Lara, but the more he crossed out and rewrote what he had written, the more did the Lara of his poems and notebooks grow away from her living prototype, from the Lara who was Katya's mother, the Lara who was away on a journey with her daughter.

The reason for this correcting and rewriting was his search for strength and exactness of .expression, but it also corresponded to the promptings of an inward reticence which forbade him to expose his personal experiences and the real events in his past with too much freedom, lest he should offend or wound those who had directly taken part in them. As a result, the steaming heat of reality was driven out of his poems and so far from their becoming morbid and devitalized, there appeared in them a broad piece of reconciliation which lifted the particular to the level of the universal and accessible to all. This was not a goal which he was consciously striving for; it came of its own accord as a consolation, like a message sent to him by Lara from her travels, like a distant greeting from her, *like her image in a dream* or the touch of her hand on his forehead, and he rejoiced at this ennobling of his verse.

I have italicized the phrase in the prose which seems to bring it closest to the experience of the poetry. But there is much here that is of more importance. In particular, 'No matter the world's unpitying heart' looks quite different from this vantage-point: the poet is able to say this, not only because the image of the loved woman is engraved on his heart indelibly, but because that image has become universalized so as to take up into itself all the woes of others. And thus the poet need no longer take account of the world's ruthlessness, only because he takes account continually of the world's victims, as typified and embodied in the one he loves. There is no question, after all, of withdrawal into the privately inviolate.

And indeed, if we are only attentive enough, the poem says this on its own account, without help from the prose gloss. For the point of the metaphor of the engraving on the heart (in itself a faded conceit out of common stock) is not so much the indelibility of the image as what the next quatrain goes on to say—how the image personifies 'humility', all the long-suffering meekness in existence.

One last observation. If Zhivago were a poet of flesh and blood, instead of a created fiction, one could say with some confidence what, as it is, one may only surmise—that the particular circumstances which attend the dream-image are drawn, probably at a subconscious level, from the adventitious juxtaposition in the poet's buried experience, of Lara's face with faces of stone. Chapter Thirteen is entitled 'Opposite the House of Caryatids', as if to emphasize how Lara's rooms in Yuryatin look across the street to the house with curiously carved human figures which have been described earlier. But it is in the 16th section of Chapter Nine that Zhivago remembers how Lara had responded to his attempt to break off his association with her, so as to return to his wife:

Lara had realized how unhappy he felt and had no wish to upset him further by a painful scene. She tried to listen to him as calmly as she could. They were talking in one of the empty front rooms, tears were running down her cheeks, but she was no more conscious of them than the stone statues on the house across the road felt the rain running down their faces. She kept saying softly: 'Do as you think best, don't worry about me. I'll get over it.' She was saying it sincerely, without any false generosity, and as she did not know that she was crying, she did not wipe away her tears.

If the dream-image of Lara in the poem is running with water and condensations and melted snow, rather than relate this to any etymological pun on her name (Lara = Larissa = the sea), I would connect it with this image of an earlier attempted separation of the lovers, and with the humility of Lara's demeanour on that occasion. To make the face of flesh approximate to a face of stone acts on our imaginations so as to idealize and universalize the particular, in the way which Pasternak says that Zhivago attempted and attained.

Notes to 'Christmas Star'

D. D. Obolensky has pointed out that this poem must be related to a passage from the early autobiography *Safe Conduct*, in which Pasternak, remembering a visit to Venice, is led on from that, by no very natural connection, to reflect on the various versions of Christmas which co-exist in his imagination:

There is a special Christmas Tree East, the East of the pre-Raphaelites. There is the presentation of the starry night according to the legend of the worship of the Magi. There is the age-old Christmas relief: the top of a gilded walnut sprinkled with blue paraffin.

The last sentence I take to be a mannered allusion to the Christmas of the children's party, with its traditional toys and curios. If so, the part of the poem most directly anticipated here is the curiously affecting quatrain which begins, 'All the quiver of candlelight, all festoons'. In these four lines, as in the six which precede them, about 'a strange glamour', Pasternak is an impenitent modernist: the strangeness of the vision is in its cubist perspective which juxtaposes three or four incompatible series of images and landscapes. Museums and art-collections provide one series of Christmas images, fairies and wizards another, aspirations after peace on earth another, children and Christmas trees yet another; by locking each series in with all the others, the poem presents a composite Christmas, a factually impossible scene compounded of all the different Christmases available to the imagination.

This is worth insisting upon because Pasternak's

revulsion from his earlier writings at the time of *Doctor Zhivago* has been eagerly interpreted, by those with an anti-modernist axe to grind, as a condemnation of the modern movement in European poetry by one who has been a leading light of that movement. But 'Christmas Star' shows that, however thoroughly by this time Pasternak was out of love with a poetic sophistication parading itself, he was not ready to abandon poetic structures which post-symbolist practice had made possible. And those who interpret Pasternak's change of heart more narrowly still, as a return to regular metres and regular rhyme-schemes, may be assured that this version reproduces faithfully the waywardness of the original in these respects. Moreover, in this poem as in others, the use I make of approximate and consciously imperfect rhymes goes very little further than Pasternak's practice.

In this poem, however, the poet seems to emphasize these features in order to achieve a deliberately rough-hewn effect. For if in certain lines the Christmas of the children's party is evoked, and other Christmases also, the framework of the poem as a whole is what *Safe Conduct* calls 'the East of the pre-Raphaelites'. By 'pre-Raphaelites' Pasternak means, of course, not any English painters of the nineteenth century, but Italians of the fifteenth. And in the poem the placing of the Nativity in a rocky cave recalls the identical odd convention used by so-called primitives of the quattrocento, such as Ghirlandaio. This deliberately 'primitive' image calls for off-rhymes, changes of metrical pattern, and uneven blocks of lines so that the poem shall be in keeping, equally 'primitive' all through.

This is corroborated by a passage in Chapter Three of Doctor Zhivago which others have remarked as bearing very directly on this poem. In the 10th section of this chapter the young Zhivago, who has promised one of his friends an article on Blok for a student paper, is driving a sleigh with his future wife Tonya through the frost-bound Moscow streets. Their destination is that Christmas party at the Sventitskys' which gives a title to Chapter Three as a whole:

It occurred to him that Blok was a manifestation of Christmas in the life and art of modern Russia—Christmas in the life of this northern city, Christmas underneath the starry skies of its modern streets and round the lighted trees in its twentieth-century drawing rooms. There was no need to write an article on Blok, he thought, all you needed do was to paint a Russian version of a Dutch Adoration of the Magi with snow in it, and wolves and a dark fir forest.

Italian or Dutch, hardly matters; what matters is the precious naivete of a primitive artist who, undeterred by considerations of historical and geographical accuracy, makes over the landscape, the personages, and the actions of the Nativity story into terms immediately familiar to himself and his fellows. This naïvete, the vividness of apprehension not joined to any sense of needful subordination of detail, gets into the poem in, for instance, the observation that some of the Wise Men's donkeys were smaller than others. And there is a corresponding, equally poignant naivete, but in literary not painterly terms, when angels and shepherds announce themselves with one voice to Mary; we are relied upon not to

ask superfluous questions about who was the spokes-
man, or when and how the shepherds came to terms
with their immaterial companions.

With this passage from Chapter Three we necessarily turn from considering 'Christmas Star' as a
poem by Pasternak, to thinking of it as a poem by
Zhivago. Does this make any difference? It does,
undoubtedly; for it compels us to take seriously the
possibility that this is indeed the poem which the
young Zhivago imagined he might write—a poem,
that is, which stands in place of an essay about
Alexander Blok, in other words a poem about
Blok.

One should notice first a crucial detail which
establishes the poem as Zhivago's, not Pasternak's:

> Across the sheeted snow-field, mica-bright,
> Led round a hut the prints of naked feet.
> About these prints, as to flame of a candle-end
> Padded and shifted sheep-dogs in the starlight.

Are flames at candle-ends more disturbing to sheep-
dogs than other kinds of flames? If not, then the simile
which alludes to them seems quite gratuitous. And
yet it is nothing less than Zhivago's signature to his
poem. This we realize only if we have noticed how,
through the sixteen chapters of prose narrative, candles
have come to have for Zhivago an occult and momentous significance such as they have for no one else but
Lara. Nowhere in the narrative are the clues to this
sown so thickly as in the pages just before and after
Zhivago's reflections about Blok and Christmas.
Throughout 'Christmas party at the Sventitskys' the
point about lighted candles is hammered home with

an insistence almost heavy-handed. The passage about 'a Dutch Adoration of the Magi' goes on:

As they drove through Kamerger Street Yury noticed that a candle had melted a patch in the icy crust on one of the windows. *Its light seemed to fall into the street as deliberately as a glance, as if the flame were keeping a watch on the passing carriages and waiting for someone.*

'A candle burned on the table, a candle burned . . .' he whispered to himself—the confused, formless beginning of a poem; he hoped that it would take shape of itself, but nothing more came to him.

As we know from a few pages before, this candle which Zhivago sees was burning in the room where Lara had just given a crucial interview to her future husband, and at the end of the novel Zhivago's dead body lies in the same room. Pasternak is so little concerned with verisimilitude in the normal tradition of the realistic novel, that on the contrary he contrives such webs of unlikely coincidence specifically so as to advise the reader not to look for the significances of realism, but for meanings of another kind. And the meaning of 'candle' is surely spelt out for us in the sentence I have ventured to italicize. That meaning is, or is to become, extremely important—as appears from the way in which, not just 'Christmas Star', but another poem also, 'Winter Night' (its refrain here anticipated), leans heavily and explicitly on these sentences of the prose.

And yet the significance of 'flame of a candle-end' *is* realistic, in this important sense: that without something of the sort there could not be a faithful and complete account of what poetic composition is, and how it works. One of Pasternak's aims in *Doctor*

Zhivago is to give such an account. And he gives it in the only way possible for exact fidelity and comprehensiveness—that is, by a working model; by making Zhivago a poet and showing how his poems come to him. Zhivago, like other poets, is influenced by some images of a private, even obsessive kind; and 'candle' is the example which Pasternak endows him with, of images of this kind. By a brilliant finesse Pasternak is able to show his poet drawing on associations of a wholly private kind, and at the same time to avoid the impenetrable obscurity which normally is inescapable in such writing.

The point to be made in calling the candle-end Zhivago's signature is that this reference establishes 'Christmas Night' as the work of a certain man who envisaged an account of Blok in the shape of a primitive Nativity-painting. And this means that the presence of Alexander Blok, in this poem where he is never named, is something to be looked for.

To establish his presence beyond cavil would require an exhaustive essay on Blok, his life, and his writings. One may think first of Blok's iconoclastic and glancing treatment of a Scriptural theme in his most famous poem, 'The Twelve', where the twelve apostles figure as a patrol of Bolshevik riflemen roaming the streets during the Revolution. But Zhivago could have known of this poem neither at the time of the Sventitskys' party, nor when he wrote 'Christmas Star'. In Chapter Fourteen we learn that 'Christmas Star' had been composed before Zhivago's return to Varykino, though it was there first committed to paper (and modified in the process). On the other hand Blok's *Italian Verses* (1909) include both an

Annunciation and an Assumption; and it may have been these that Zhivago had in mind when he wrote his Nativity for Blok's sake. In the second place 'the wind over the steppe' should be compared with 'The Wind. Four Fragments about Blok', among Pasternak's poems published after *Doctor Zhivago*. What these four splendid lyrics appear to say is that Blok was no 'civic' or 'moral' poet, to be taken up into a national tradition, but amoral as the wind, as ambiguous as that natural force, and incidentally as destructive.

For this, it seems to me, is the most important aspect of Blok to be remembered in this connection: the extent to which his achievement, in other poems besides 'The Twelve', lay in his grasp, from the start and from before the start, of the essential ambiguity in the Revolution—a convulsion as of physical nature, at once a liberating renascence and a fury of cruel destruction. Though translators have unaccountably obscured the fact by suppressing for instance the reference to arson in one of Zhivago's quatrains about the blazing of the new star, a great deal of the power in his treatment comes of his seeing the even greater historical convulsion of the Nativity just as Blok saw the Revolution, as ambiguous, at once tender and appalling. These quatrains seem to approach the point made by W. B. Yeats in 'The Second Coming'—that when the superhuman invades the human realm, all the human can say of it is that it is non-human; in consequence, from the human standpoint the super-human will always be confused with the subhuman, the bestial with the divine.

These connections with Blok may seem tenuous.

But in the first poem of the sequence, as in virtually all which follow 'Christmas Star', the office of the poet is likened to, or even identified with, the role of Christ. Seeming to see allusions to Blok in 'Christmas Star' one is only detecting the same train of feeling; with the difference that the poetic office is here filled not by Zhivago but by the greatest Russian poet of the generation before his. Moreover, what is the alternative? Is 'Christmas Star' no more than a touching and accomplished pastiche? What happens, on any other reading, to those insistences in the prose-clue about 'the life and art of *modern* Russia', 'its *modern* streets', 'its *twentieth-century* drawing rooms'? Zhivago, with of course Pasternak behind him, regards Blok as the poet who baptized Russian poetry into the present century. For Russians this was a baptism of fire as for no others. Would there be impiety, or disproportion even, in a Russian's comparing the convulsion of the Revolution with the convulsion which began at Bethlehem and ended at Calvary? Or with his seeing, in the one great Russian poet who in his maturity lived through the Revolution and came to terms with it in his art, an analogue of the Redeemer?

Notes to 'Daybreak'

This is hard to translate. The baldly assertive style seems to lay claim to sublime perceptions which it does not bother to earn; more than in most of Zhivago's poems, the poetry is in the spaces between the quatrains, more than in the verses themselves.

According to George Katkov, there is Pasternak's

authority for saying that the 'you' addressed in the first stanzas is Christ. Accordingly Katkov believes that the poem deals directly with what Pasternak described as his own condition following 'an illumination which came over the poet in the first months of World War II'; thereafter he described himself as 'an atheist who has lost his faith'.

Realizing the need to relate the poem not only to Pasternak's life but more immediately to Zhivago's, Katkov decides (*In the Interlude*, tr. Kamen, p. 236): 'The poem relates to the last part of Zhivago's life . . . when he shared his room with the peasant painter Vasya.' This is the period when Zhivago publishes 'his views on medicine, his definitions of health and sickness, reflections on evolution and the mutation of species, his theory of personality as the biological basis of the organism, and thoughts about religion and history (his views had much in common with those of his uncle and Sima) . . .' And bearing heavily on this last clue, Katkov would have it that a main source for the poem is the same as that for the Magdalen poems which are to follow—that is to say, in the 17th section of Chapter Thirteen, the homily which, overheard by Zhivago, Sima Tuntseva delivers to Lara.

The trouble is that no one would arrive at this reading from a study of the poem by itself or in its place in the sequence. Undoubtedly Pasternak's statement of his intentions is illuminating; but it leaves open to question how far the intentions have been fulfilled. For instance, 'All night I have read your will' is inexplicable, until Pasternak's testimony reveals that what is meant is reading the Gospels; but what reader would arrive at that solution, with nothing to go on but what the poem itself provides?

We owe it to Pasternak, if not to Zhivago, to think that over and above this secret meaning he provided another, more superficial, which still hangs together and holds the attention. The first line in itself promises a love-poem. And though it's true that the next few lines cannot be made to fit Zhivago's relations with any of the women in his life, the piece can still be read as a love-poem all through. Moreover I believe that this was intended by the author. For in his autobiography *Safe Conduct* Pasternak invokes many of the distinctive images of this poem, when speaking of the effects of a youthful love-affair in Marburg:

I was surrounded by transformed objects. Something never before experienced crept into the substance of reality. Morning recognized my face and seemed to have come to be with me and never to leave me . . . Gradually the town began to move. Carts, bicycles, vans and trains began slithering in all directions. Above them like invisible plumes serpentined human plans and designs. They wreathed and moved with the compression of very close allegories which are understood without explanations. Birds, houses and dogs, trees and horses, tulips and people became shorter and more disconnected than when childhood had known them. The laconic freshness of life was revealed to me, it crossed the street, took me by the hand and led me along the pavement.[1]

Love for a woman, love for God . . . It would be foolish to think that if the poem is about the one, it

[1] *Safe Conduct*, tr. by Beatrice Scott. *Boris Pasternak. The Collected Prose Works*, ed. by S. Schimanski (London, 1945), pp. 76–7.

cannot be about the other. On the contrary there is a massive tradition of regarding the one as a paradigm of the other, especially when it leads, as it does in the poem, into the widest possible dispersal of sympathy among all modes of being. And thus there is no need to exclude George Katkov's observation that 'In "Daybreak" the import of the New Testament as a whole for modern metropolitan urban conditions is revealed.'

Notes to 'The Miracle'

It is disconcerting that when Zhivago gives this account of a specific instance of that 'wonder-working' which he referred to in the poem 'August', the miracle he chooses to write of is not a blessing but a curse, where the wonder-working power expresses itself not in creation but in annihilation. To be sure the poem makes provision for the instructive moral which commentators draw from the corresponding passages in Scripture: a sterile self-sufficiency is always evil, we must fructify in help and sympathy for others. But important as this precept is in Zhivago's scheme of things, it would be wrong, I believe, to think this the point of the whole poem: for these are religious or metaphysical poems, only incidentally ethical. And in the sequence as a whole, considered as a sustained religious meditation, one reason for 'The Miracle' is not hard to find: for the disconcerting shock it gives should prepare us for the note of sombre exultation at the end of 'Gethsemane', and thus of the whole sequence, where Christ, the doomed god, glories in his unimpaired omnipotence.

129

In other words, the God whom Zhivago gives us is at least as much the God of the Old Testament as of the New: the emphasis at the end is far more on a God of Power than a God of Love. And this is one way to explain why he chose, from among the miracles in the New Testament, this incident of the barren fig-tree, where Christ's action has a sort of primitive ferocity.

However, the poem departs in interesting ways from the account given, for instance, by St. Mark. In the first place, where Mark puts Christ in the company of his disciples, Zhivago insists that on the contrary Christ is utterly alone. And secondly, whereas in the Gospel Christ is angered by the fig-tree because he is hungry, in Zhivago's account Christ's motive is harder to define: the hunger which the fig-tree cannot allay is metaphysical.

On a casual reading it may seem that the fig-tree calls down the divine wrath because it embodies all that is desolate and sterile in the wastelands about it, and because this reflects with intolerable exactness the desolation and sterility in the traveller's soul. It is true that images of sterility and stagnation are powerfully accumulated in the first lines of the poem. But on the other hand the air is balmy over the wilderness, and it is not so much a wilderness as not to harbour lizards and (perhaps the clinching point) it has in it the sounds of gushing springs and running streams. It is not for nothing that these images of refreshment are suddenly introduced before the curse is uttered. They make it clear that the sterility which is exterminated is only partly outside the observer's mind, he brings most of it with him and

130

projects it upon his surroundings; a landscape of the mind is imposed upon, and supplants, the landscape of actuality. And this makes the story more barbaric than ever, the 'moral' even less acceptable. The unfortunate fig-tree is blasted much less for any sterility it has in itself than for a sterility in the squinting eye of the beholder. The tree is punished out of the same childish petulance with which, when we are out of sorts, we slash at dandelion-heads with a walking-stick. And what are we to make of this?

We begin to make something of it only if we attend to the untranslatable ambiguity in the word *chudo* which gives this poem its title. The word means 'miracle'; but also, more generally, 'wonder', 'marvel'. Elsewhere in the sequence, though pre-eminently here, Zhivago exploits this play of meaning in the word so as to talk, at one and the same time, of the miraculous capacities of God and of the prodigy of the poet's gift of utterance which is, so we are made to infer, no less miraculous. This ambiguity in the 'wonder-working' of an earlier poem should have prepared us to see, in the solitary traveller here, a human poet no less than an incarnate God. This poet looks to the landscapes about him (which might well be the landscapes of politics as well as physical scenery) to take him out of himself and cure his sterility by making the act of poetic utterance possible. The landscape fails him: the lizards do not move him for instance to 'bless them unawares'; of them, and the springs and streams about them, he might say, with Coleridge in another place, 'I see, not feel, how beautiful they are'. Focusing upon the fig-tree all his anger at this unhelpfulness, he after all does better than slash at a dandelion-head. For his anger finds utterance; and it does not matter that the utterance is a curse, not a blessing. For 'a miracle is a miracle, a miracle is God'. Poetry can be made from invective.

Coleridge, dejected because the springs of poetry had run dry in him, uttered his state in the great poetry of 'Dejection, an Ode', from which I have just quoted. I find it more helpful to remember this, when considering the important penultimate line, than to follow George Katkov when he says: 'Pasternak seems to think that belief in the miracles of the New Testament differs from belief in magic, because the miracle in Christian interpretation is a revelation of God's providence which occurs, not at the moments of our strength, but at times when we are dismayed and go astray.' It is surely the miracle-worker himself who is startled by the miracle when he is 'all at odds', not those he does the miracle for.

Katkov, who agrees about the ambiguity of 'miracle', goes on to say, 'There can be no doubt that Pasternak believed his own poetry to be "miraculous" in that sense.' This is surely true. But it is important to get the emphasis right. For Pasternak has been accused of 'surrendering to the irrational'; and it is important not to seem to credit him with belief in Gothic fancies such as sometimes trapped his contemporary Yeats into a sort of half-belief. Of course, to those whose idea of rationality is bounded by the anti-religious and anti-poetic rationalism of the Enlightenment, Pasternak does indeed embrace the irrational. But, I take it, he does not believe that, because he is a poet, he can blast fig-trees or raise

the dead or make the blind see—except metaphorically. Metaphorically he can do all these things; for
within the created world of a poem the creator's fiat
is absolute. In the poem he is indeed free of natural
law, free to bless and to curse at his will. He can for
instance write a book, partly in prose, partly in verse,
in which he takes it for granted that the Russian
Revolution did more harm than good. If that book
creates a world which hangs together, is recogniz-
ably close to the world we live in, and strongly moves
our sympathies, there is no appeal against the creator's verdict on the Revolution. So long as the reader
inhabits the world of that book, the Russian Revolution is for him precisely what the creator of that
book decreed that it should be. And the anger and
dismay which *Doctor Zhivago* caused to the heirs of
that Revolution shows how impossible it is to over-
look or to take lightly the sense in which indeed the
poet is a miracle-worker, the act of poetic utterance
miraculous. 'A miracle is a miracle, a miracle is God.'
Believing along these lines, Pasternak is echoing a
Renaissance thinker like Philip Sidney, for whom
poetry is the noblest human activity because it is that
activity in which man, as 'maker', most nearly ap-
proaches the creativeness of God.

What is meant by the poet's being in his poem
freed from the laws of nature is made clear by a
curious and arresting passage in the 7th section of
Chapter Twelve, 'Iced Rowanberries'. Zhivago at this
point, still in the *tayga* with the partisans, is listening
to a long rambling monologue by the woman
Kubarikha, addressing the bystanders after she has
claimed to charm infection out of a sick cow. Zhivago

realizes that some of Kubarikha's gibberish, about a woman's shoulder being cut open by a sword to reveal 'a measure of corn or a squirrel or a·honey-comb', is 'the opening passage of an ancient chron-icle, either of Novgorod or Ipatyevo, but so distorted by the errors of copyists and the repetitions of sor-cerers and bards that its original meaning had been lost'. Before long he is launched upon a grotesque day-dream about Lara's left shoulder being thus opened. But first he reflects:

No deep and strong feeling, such as we may come across here and there in the world, is unmixed with compassion. The more we love, the more the object of our love seems to us to be a victim. Occasionally, a man's compassion for a woman exceeds all measure, and his imagination removes her from the realm of possible happenings and places her in situations which are never encountered in life. He sees her at the mercy of the surrounding air, of the laws of nature and of the centuries which preceded her.

If the man in question is a poet, he saves the loved woman from the rule of the laws of nature by placing her in a poem 'in situations which are never encoun-tered in life'. A clear example of this in the poems of Zhivago is 'Rendezvous', where the dream-image of Lara comes to us first as very precisely 'at the mercy of the surrounding air' (with snow in her hair, all over her clothes, and even in her mouth), and is gradually rescued from natural law by the super-natural power of the poetic utterance about her. Once again, there is nothing of magical mumbo-jumbo about this contention: almost any European poem since Rimbaud shows the poet breaking free of

134

natural law, and, by juxtaposition of images, creating perhaps a time in which Nineveh and New York are contemporaneous. The miraculous power of poetry is thus not an article of faith, but a plain statement of observable fact.

If the last stanza of 'The Miracle' may thus rely to some extent on Zhivago's recollections of the cow-healer Kubarikha, much more of the poem, I suggest, draws its images from a later episode of Zhivago's life, which provided material also for the poem 'Indian Summer'. This is in the 2nd section of Chapter Fifteen, where Zhivago is toiling slowly back to Moscow through countryside ravaged and depopulated by Civil War. To be sure, that country is by no means sterile; on the contrary it is strangled by its own fertility, now that no people are left to crop it—and, as I have argued, this is the central matter of 'Indian Summer'. On the other hand the image of the sun scorching the herbage is common to both poems and to the passage of prose; and there is what I am prepared to think a deliberate echo, in 'a few clouds raggedly followed':

Everything was in ceaseless, slow, measured movement: the flowing river, the road running to meet it and Yury walking along the road in the same direction as the clouds. Nor were the rye fields motionless. Something stirred in them, something which filled them from end to end with a small incessant rummaging and which nauseated Yury.

Never had there been such a plague of mice. They had bred in unbelievable multitudes such as had never been seen before. They scurried over Yury's face and hands and inside his sleeves and trousers at night when he was caught by darkness and forced to spend the night in the open; they raced across the road by day, gorged and teeming, and turned into squeaking, pulsing slush when they were trodden underfoot.

The nausea that Zhivago feels for the mice, nature-poet as he is, is the nearest he comes to uttering a curse on the natural order. Moreover he is alone, travelling to the town, Moscow, where he will fore-gather with those who figure as his by no means staunch disciples, Gordon and Dudorov. (The passage immediately precedes Zhivago's meeting with a disciple who for a time is more loyal, Vassya Brykin.) One other reason why 'The Miracle' deserves its place is that it reveals Zhivago as a nature-poet certainly, with love and veneration for the natural creation; but, unlike a nature-poet such as Wordsworth, he realizes that his art of utterance ultimately transcends the natural and must, if necessary, do it violence.

Notes to 'Earth'

The best note to this poem is a comment by Henry Gifford (*Poetry*, May 1962, p. 125): 'Pasternak and his contemporaries may have been restless as were poets everywhere half a century back. They tried new metres; they revolutionized rhyme; they extended the language. However, their situation wasn't that of American and English poets: they had not to face the full urban paralysis of feeling and language. The Russian city, even today, keeps touch with nature.' This is not just what Zhivago's poem takes for granted; it is also, in part, what his poem says.

But another thing it seems to say is that in a society

vowed to thorough-going renovation, to optimistic spring-cleaning, the poet's task is to recollect how there is a tragic, irremediable dimension to life—a dimension which the non-human Creation reminds him about. For the images appear to come to Zhivago out of the period of his short-lived enthusiasm for the Revolution, when he was at Melyuzeyevo. It was there (Chapter Five, section six) that 'the houses and fences huddled closer together in the dusk'. And it is there (section eight) that Zhivago expatiates to the Lara he as yet hardly knows:

Last night I was watching the meeting in the square. It was an astonishing sight. Mother Russia is on the move, she can't stand still, she's restless and she can't find rest, she's talking and she can't stop. And it isn't as if only people were talking. Stars and trees meet and converse, flowers talk philosophy at night, stone houses hold meetings. It's like something out of the Gospels, don't you think? Like in the days of the apostles . . .

Lara responds,

I know what you mean about stars and trees holding meetings. I understand that. It's happened to me too.

But Lara (and this is surely central to the irreplaceable value she comes to have for Zhivago) has lived in the tragic dimension since long before. For Zhivago expostulates: 'And then, in the midst of all this general rejoicing, I come up against your puzzlingly sad, absent look . . .' (At this point in the novel Lara and 'Mother Russia' are almost the one same thing.)

Thus the friends with whom Zhivago foregathers at the end of this poem are not I think his friends of Melyuzeyevo days, but rather (to take Henry

Gifford's hint) his fellow-poets of a later period in Moscow. And their task, so the poem seems to say, is to insist, continually and unseasonably, on the irremediable because tragic aspect of human life.

Notes to 'The Bad Days'

This is a poem about Jesus; to take its place in the sequence it ought to be about Zhivago too. But at first it's not clear how Zhivago comes into it.

To be sure, there is a plain general resemblance between the atmosphere evoked by the poem and that established in the later sections of Chapter Thirteen, when Zhivago and Lara, re-united after Zhivago's escape from Siberia, are forced to move from Yuryatin to Varykino by the thickening air of suspicion, investigation and terror in the Urals town. Thus, what corresponds to the first four stanzas of the poem is Zhivago saying to Lara, in the 16th section of Chapter Thirteen:

You know it looks as if I'll be forced to resign from my jobs. It's always the same thing—it happens time and again. At first everything is splendid.—'Come along. We welcome good, honest work, we welcome ideas, especially new ideas. What could please us better? Do your work, your research, struggle, carry on.'

Then you find in practice that what they mean by ideas is nothing but words—claptrap in praise of the revolution and the regime. I'm sick and tired of it. And it's not the kind of thing I'm good at.

Certainly we should think that it is from his memory of this experience that Zhivago wrote the first four stanzas of his poem. Less certainly the sixth stanza may well derive from Lara's note, a few sentences later, about the second of the 'certain regular stages' which the regime goes through:

Then comes the second stage. The accent is all on the dark forces, the false sympathizers, the hangers-on. There is more and more suspicion—informers, intrigues, hatreds. You are perfectly right that we are entering on the second stage.

And undoubtedly relevant is Komarovsky of all people, in the 1st section of Chapter Fourteen, telling Zhivago: 'You are a mockery of that whole world, an insult to it.'

But, while we must stop short of looking for the one-to-one correspondences of allegory, I think we have the right to look for more than this general analogy. We have the right to ask, for instance: What was Zhivago's temptation in the desert? And part of the answer might be in the 3rd section of Chapter Thirteen, where Zhivago is reading the proclamations posted on the House of Caryatids in Yuryatin. He reflects:

Only once in his life had this uncompromising language and single-mindedness filled him with enthusiasm. Was it possible that he must pay for that one moment of rash enthusiasm all his life by never hearing, year after year, anything but these unchanging, shrill, crazy exclamations and demands, ever more lifeless, meaningless, and unfulfillable as time went by? Was it possible that in one short moment of over-sensitive generosity he had allowed himself to be enslaved for ever?

Of course it was not possible, as the narrative and poems alike show. And in fact Zhivago's initial sympathy with the Revolution is so short-lived, and sketched in so lightly, that while it may present itself to him as a surrender, to the reader it figures only as a sway towards a temptation which is then vigorously resisted.

In any case, as J. M. Cohen rightly says,[1] 'Pharisaism, not the Revolution, was the enemy, because it was remorselessly destructive of creative energy.' And the passage just quoted is only one of many in which Pharisaism is seen as above all, whether in its Revolutionary guise or some other, a vice of language, of language that is lifeless, meaningless, shrill. Unless we recognize with Pasternak that the shrillness of language pulled loose of meaning is a vice which infects every department of corporate life, we shall see his and Zhivago's apotheosis of the poet, the artist in language, as merely megalomania, or else as the symptom of a historical phase of thinking on these matters which went out for us with Oscar Wilde And this would be to evade the challenge of *Doctor Zhivago* altogether.

But finally, what in Zhivago's experience corresponds to the miracle alluded to in the last stanza? Both Eugene Kayden and Henry Kamen, in their versions of this poem, name Lazarus in the last line; where Zhivago's poem does not name him at all. To name him is to make the poem wholly about Jesus, not about Zhivago at all. And it is to shut out all memory, for instance, of a passage from the 2nd section of Chapter Nine:

I love the warm, dry winter breath of the cellar, the smell of earth, roots and snow that hits you the moment

[1] J. M. Cohen, 'Servant to the Ages'. *The Spectator*, April 6th, 1962.

you raise the trap, as you go down in the early hours before the winter dawn, a weak, flickering light in your hand.

It is true that the word for 'cellar' is not the same—in the prose it is 'pogreb', in the verse 'podval';[1] but on the other hand there is an echo in the word for a candle going out—in the prose 'oogasnoot', in the verse 'gasla'. And the point of recollecting the prose is that there the cellar which Zhivago descends to is used for the storing of vegetables through the winter, of twenty sacks of potatoes, of 'two barrels of salted cucumbers and two of sauerkraut prepared by Tonya', of 'carrots buried in dry sand, and radishes and beet and turnips'.

For 'resurrection' or, as I translate it here, 'the risen', is not used by Zhivago solely to refer to human life. On the contrary it is as often as not vegetable life that he has first in mind. We have already encountered in the sequence one poem, 'Indian Summer', which turns wholly on the business of bottling and pickling and preserving; and when, in the last section of Chapter Six, the elusive and omnipotent Yevgraf advises Tonya to retreat to the Urals, he speaks particularly of the vegetables she will grow

[1] 'Podval', however, occurs elsewhere in the prose, and in a context not without significance. This is in the third section of Chapter Seven, where Zhivago and his father-in-law are allowed for the first and last time into one of the state stores reserved for the privileged. This is in a cellar: 'They came out of the vault intoxicated, not by the mere thought of food, but by the consciousness that they too were of use in the world and did not live in vain, and had deserved the praise and thanks which Tonya would shower on them at home.' This too is the experience of a sort of 'resurrection'.

141

there, and of the valuable earthiness of that environ-
ment.

How crucial this is comes out when J. M. Cohen
can assert (*The Spectator*, loc. cit.) that Pasternak sees
Christ 'not in His office of Redeemer—for with this
aspect of Christ's mission Pasternak, being by birth a
Jew, did not identify himself—but in that of the
Suffering Servant, prefigured in Isaiah'. Pasternak's
Christ is certainly the Redeemer to the extent that
he is repeatedly associated, or even identified, with
earth and growth from the earth, for instance in
'In Holy Week' and at the end of 'Magdalene II'
as well as here. The act of preserving vegetable life,
through from autumn to spring, is an exact, homely
image for the Redeemer's promise of resurrection
from the grave. The autobiography, *Safe Conduct*,
published in 1931, shows how constant for Pasternak
was the association of Resurrection with vegetable
life stored in cellars. The subject of this ornate prose
by the younger Pasternak is the cellar of a florist and
the scent of the flowers stored there:

Their sweet never-coughed-through breath filled the
wide rim of the trapdoor from the cellar's depths. They
covered one's chest with a kind of wooded pleurisy. This
scent reminded one of something and then slipped away,
duping one's consciousness. It seemed that a conception
about the earth which the spring months composed on
the theme of this scent, encouraged them to return year
by year, and that the sources of the Greek belief in Demeter
were somewhere very near at hand.[1]

---

[1] *Safe Conduct*, tr. Beatrice Scott. *Boris Pasternak. The
Collected Prose Works*, ed. Stefan Schimanski (London, 1945),
p. 59.

Notes to 'Magdalene I'

I have been compelled in my translation to take more liberties than I like, notably with the order of images inside each stanza.

The most obvious source for this poem in Zhivago's experience is the conversation which he overhears, in the 17th section of Chapter Thirteen, between Sima Tuntseva and Lara. This is less a conversation than a monologue or informal homily by the eccentric Sima, on the liturgical texts for Easter in the Orthodox Church. Two passages are particularly relevant. The first is where Sima says:

It has always interested me that Mary Magdalene is mentioned on the very eve of Easter, on the threshold of the death and resurrection of Christ. I don't know the reason for it, but this reminder seems to me so timely at the moment of his taking leave of life and before he takes it up again. Now look at the way the reminder is made—what genuine passion there is in it and what a ruthless directness.

Passion and ruthless directness are what the translator finds in the poem, and must do his best to reproduce in English. However, Zhivago's poem takes for its point of departure a more specific observation by Sima, on a particular passage from the liturgy, in which the Magdalen must be imagined as speaking:

Again she grieves in a terribly tangible way over her past and over the corruption which it rooted in her, so that every night it comes to life in her once more. 'The flaring up of lust is to me like night, the dark, moonless zeal of sin.'

The terrible tangibility is certainly taken over and pushed even further by this poem which moves from one image of squalid prostitution to another. In the shocking and extremely powerful image of Eternity as the harlot's client (the word is 'vechnost', which has ominous overtones of 'oblivion', to qualify the more consolatory ring of English 'eternity'), this word 'eternity' should not be narrowed down to merely a name for Christ; yet since Christ to any sort of Christian embodies eternity, undoubtedly at one level of apprehension the harlot's customer is Christ himself, perhaps in a quite literal and physical sense. And thus in the last stanza, though the expressions 'between my knees' and 'strain into my body' doubtless build up in the first place a traditional statuesque image, of the Marys cradling and comforting the body of Christ as it is brought down from the cross, they cannot help but carry also a defiantly erotic meaning; and this means that there may even be deliberate phallic overtones to the reference to the shaft of the cross. This sustained ambiguity rather plainly has something to do with a digression which Sima makes in her homily, on the ambiguity of the Russian word 'strast', an ambiguity to which fortunately there is an exact analogy in English, between the theological and the erotic sense of the word 'passion'. Sima at this point is confessing her lack of sympathy for the ascetic and self-mortifying side of Christian doctrine and practice.

All the same, this element in the poem should be acknowledged only in passing. It is present but very much subordinate. As regards erotic 'passion', for instance, Sima's objection to the ascetic's fascination with it is on the score of vulgarity. And no reader of the poem can afford to ignore Lara's impatience with it when in Chapter Fifteen, bowed over Zhivago's corpse, she reflects upon their mutual love:

It was not out of necessity that they loved each other, 'enslaved by passion', as lovers are described. They loved each other because everything around them willed it, the trees and the clouds and the sky over their heads and the earth under their feet. Perhaps their surrounding world, the strangers they met in the street, the landscapes drawn up for them to see on their walks, the rooms in which they lived or met, were even more pleased with their love than they were themselves.

What saves Pasternak's narrative from the trite tastelessness of the *'grande passion'* is this insistence that the pleasure his lovers took in each other spilled over on to (the progression is significant) first, other people, then landscapes and the natural, and last, utilitarian artefacts like 'rooms'

It is more important to realize that this is the point in the sequence of poems at which the identification of Zhivago with Christ is made inescapable.[1] To put it more exactly, since the poem is Zhivago's rather than Pasternak's, this is the point where Zhivago brings himself to face the possibility of this identification, and to take on the responsibility of it. In the immediately preceding poems, 'The Miracle', 'The

---

[1] In *Literaturnaya Gazeta* for October 25th, 1958, five Russian critics pointed out that 'Zhivago's entire path through life is consistently likened to "the Lord's passion" in the Gospels'. I cannot agree with D. D. Obolensky (in *Slavonic and East European Review*, December 1961) that there is 'some exaggeration' in this claim.

Earth', and 'The Bad Days', the reader has seen
Zhivago's experience and Christ's experience steadily
converging; and I think we should believe that the
fact of this convergence dawns on Zhivago himself
only as it dawns on his reader. It is something which
he finds it harder and harder not to recognize; and
in the Magdalen poems he recognizes the fact and all
its implications. He recognizes and accepts his own
identity with Christ by recognizing how inevitable,
from Lara's point of view, is her own identity with
Mary Magdalene. This has been abundantly prepared
for in the prose narrative, perhaps nowhere more
explicitly than in the third section of Chapter Fourteen, where Lara says, 'Yury, darling, you are my
strength and my refuge, God forgive me the blas-
phemy.' Undoubtedly we should take it that this
experience, of being addressed in words which had
been addressed to Christ, is one of the things which
enable Zhivago to write this poem. What need he had,
of all the help he could get, will emerge if we consider
that the poem is a prophetic vision by Zhivago of
what Lara will feel when she bows above his own
dead body. For this is indeed the case: the poem
describes much the same arc of feeling as Lara has
experienced in the 15th and 16th sections of Chapter
Fifteen. For instance, the only adequate gloss on the
last stanza is surely this, from the account of Lara's
feelings when she was alone with Zhivago's corpse:

This it was that had brought them happiness and liberation in those days. Knowledge, not from the head, but
warm knowledge imparted to each other, instinctive,
immediate.

Such knowledge filled her now, a dark, indistinct knowledge of death, a preparedness for death which removed all helplessness in its presence. It was as if she had lived twenty lives, and had lost Yury countless times, and had accumulated such experience of the heart in this domain that everything she felt and did beside this coffin was exactly right and to the point.

Once Mary Magdalene is identified with Lara, a whole new series of references from the prose are taken up into Zhivago's poem. For instance, the guilt and shame which Lara feels when alone with the dead Zhivago is not at all for sexual promiscuity and abandonment in her past, but (as we learn later) for having deserted the child she had by Zhivago. (At the risk of being schematically allegorical in my reading, I am prepared to think that this lost child may 'stand for' the earlier poems by Pasternak which we know he repudiated with contumely by the time he wrote *Doctor Zhivago*.) On the other hand the narrative has by no means shirked from indicating that Lara is lustful. The power and conviction of Lara's portrayal as early as Chapter Two comes from the acknowledgment that when she was seduced in adolescence this was no accident, that something in her responded to the voluptuary in her seducer: 'A tired smile puckered her eyes and loosened her lips, but in answer to his amused glance she gave him a sly wink of complicity.' And in the 5th section of the next chapter we are told explicitly how she could lose herself in 'the nightmare of sensuality which terrified her whenever she awoke from it'. It is these touches which make of Lara's seduction something more interesting and credible, and thus more affecting, than the stereotype of the pure and passive virgin cruelly violated. One might agree with Stuart Hampshire (in *Encounter*, November 1958) that 'The villain is an abstract sketch of bourgeois corruption', but certainly not when he adds, 'and the story of his relation with the heroine is mere melodrama'.

In Chapter Thirteen the point is made all over again that there is something in Lara which responds to Komarovsky, her original seducer. In the 12th section of this chapter Zhivago gets Lara to acknowledge that this is so:

He is the man of whom I shall always be incurably, insanely jealous.

How can you say such a thing? Don't you see, it isn't just that I don't love him, I despise him.

Can you know yourself as well as that? Human nature is so mysterious and so full of contradictions. Perhaps there is something in your very loathing of him that keeps you bound to him more surely than to any man whom you love of your own free will, without compulsion.

What a terrible thing to say! And as usual, the way you put it makes me feel that this thing, monstrous and unnatural as it is, is perhaps true . . .

We must surely think that if Zhivago had not wrung this admission out of Lara he would not have started a poem which is put as much into her mouth as into Mary Magdalene's, by making her confess to 'the flaring up of lust . . . the dark, moonless zeal of sin'.

In the sequence of these poems, Zhivago's identifying of himself with Christ depends upon, and is validated by, the identification of Lara with the

Magdalen. And this means that there is at least one other beam of light which must be allowed to fall from the prose narrative on this poem. For what is it in Zhivago's death which Lara, as the Magdalen figure, recognizes as divine? In the 16th section of Chapter Fifteen Lara speaks to the dead Zhivago:

Think of it! Again something just our kind, just up our street. Your going, that's the end of me. Again something big, inescapable. The riddle of life, the riddle of death, the beauty of genius, the beauty of loving . . .

The unexpected item in this catalogue is 'the beauty of genius'. It seems that for Lara—and so by implication for us, and for Zhivago himself—what makes Zhivago identical with Christ is above all his capacity as an artist.

Notes to 'Magdalene II'

Like the first poem about the Magdalen, this too leans very heavily on the 17th section of Chapter Thirteen, where the mildly dotty Sima Tuntseva speaks to Lara about the significance of Easter in the liturgy of the Orthodox Church, with particular reference (so George Katkov says[1]) to 'a Slavonic translation of a Byzantine spiritual poet, the nun Kassia of the ninth century'. (In Chapter Fifteen we learn, of Zhivago's own 'philosophy of life', adumbrated in booklets published after his return to Moscow, that 'his views had much in common with those of his uncle and Sima'.)

[1] G. Katkov, in *Pasternak. In the Interlude*, tr. by H. Kamen (Paperback Edn., p. 133).

At the same time of course the identifications of Zhivago with Christ and of Lara with Mary Magdalene are by this time so firmly established that it's impossible not to think of the point, much later in the novel. where Lara, alone with Zhivago's corpse, communes with him and speaks to him.

The most relevant passage from Sima's commentary appears to be her gloss on a passage from the liturgy for either Tuesday or Wednesday of Passion Week:

She begs Christ to accept her tears of repentance and be moved by the sincerity of her signs, so that she may dry His most pure feet with her hair—reminding Him that in the rushing waves of her hair Eve took refuge when she was overcome with fear and shame in paradise. 'Let me kiss Thy most pure feet and water them with my tears and dry them with the hair of my head, which covered Eve and sheltered her when, her ears filled with sound, she was afraid in the cool of the day in paradise.' And immediately after all this about her hair, she exclaims: 'Who can fathom the multitude of my sins and the depth of Thy judgment?' What familiarity, what equal terms between God and life, God and the individual, God and a woman!

Nothing matters here more than that last exclamation, 'What familiarity . . .!' For there are indications also in the vocabulary of the poem that what is aimed at is a shocking, almost brutal directness of address; and plainly the translator must try to bring this over.

Thus the woman who speaks the poem, if she is Mary Magdalene, is also Eve, and certainly she is Lara. Nor should we exclude J. M. Cohen's perception[1] that 'the repentant Magdalene seems to represent the poet's unredeemed nature: what he would in fact have been but for the consciousness of his prophetic destiny'. For, as Cohen realizes, this gives added point to the fine poignancy by which the woman's inadequacy is revealed, the stroke of genius which makes her think, when the ground trembles at the rending of the veil of the temple, that it does so out of sympathy for *her*.

But there is another passage in the novel the relevance of which has been overlooked, though it is relevant at a more profound level and therefore more crucially. This is the 15th section of Chapter Six, which deals with Zhivago's attack of typhus in Moscow, after his return from the front but before he retreats with his family to the Urals. In delirium Zhivago dreams that he is writing a poem:

The subject of his poem was neither the entombment nor the resurrection but the days between; the title was 'Turmoil'.

He had always wanted to describe how for three days the black, raging, worm-filled earth had assailed the deathless incarnation of love, storming it with rocks and rubble—as waves fly and leap at a sea coast, cover and submerge it—how for three days the black hurricane of earth rages, advancing and retreating.

This astonishing feat of bizarre imagination gets into the last stanza of the poem in the no less astonishing word which I have translated 'ram'—the word 'stolknoot', for which the dictionary gives 'collide (with)'.

[1] J. M. Cohen, 'Servant to the Ages'. *The Spectator*, April 6th, 1962.

What is most important, however, about this passage from Chapter Six is that in Zhivago's delirium the writing of his poem ('He was writing what he should have written long ago and had always wished to write, but never could') is tied up very closely with the figure of his half-brother Yevgraf. And indeed, as Edmund Wilson has realized, no other passage gives clearer clues to the significance of this mysterious figure:

He knew for certain that this boy was the spirit of his death or, to put it quite plainly, that he was his death. Yet how could he be his death if he was helping him to write a poem? How could death be useful, how was it possible for death to be a help?

This of course is the very question which the Crucifixion poses for Mary Magdalene near the end of this poem. And the answer she finds in the last stanza is the answer which Zhivago finds in Chapter Six when, after talking of 'the black hurricane of earth', he passes the crisis in his illness:

Two lines kept coming into his head: 'We are glad to be near you' and 'Time to wake up'.

Near him, touching him, were hell, corruption, dissolution, death; yet equally near him were the spring and Mary Magdalene and life.—And it was time to awake. Time to awake and to get up. Time to arise, time for the resurrection.

The sudden introduction of the name of the Magdalen, at this stage in the novel where Lara's identification with her has not yet been established, seems to point very deliberately to this poem, and to the placing of 'resurrection' in its last line as in the last word of this section of the prose. And thus the reader who wants to reduce the poem, to internalize its drama by changing its metaphysical terms into psychological ones, can do so; he can read the Magdalen's prophetic complaint to Christ on the cross as the complaint of one of a man's selves to his other self, as he foresees, and undergoes in imagination, the ordeal of an all but mortal illness.

To the question, 'How can death be useful?' the answer which the Magdalen finds at the foot of the cross, and Zhivago in his struggle with typhus, is the enigmatic paradox, 'Life-in-Death'. What brings the unrefreshing paradox home to us, as a refreshing lived experience, is chiefly the imagery which the poet finds for it:

> So much of colony, of river-run and spinney . . .

But in the poem the paradox is brought home in another way, by a deliberate double-meaning:

> Who is it for in the world, so much bounty?
> So much hurt, such a capacity?
> Is there so much of being and life in the world?
> So much of colony, of river-run and spinney?

The third line may be taken to mean: 'Is there enough human life in the world to deserve that Christ be sacrificed for it?' And this is apparently how previous translators have taken the line. But along with this reading which expects the answer No, there is surely another which expects the answer Yes. For we may take the line to mean: 'Is there (qualitatively) so much of life in the world as Christ, hanging on the cross, embodies and gathers up into Himself?' Unless this second meaning is present along with

153

the first, there is no point to 'river-run and spinney' along with 'colony'. And in fact Pasternak repeatedly shows that the resurrection which Christ brings about, as does any prophetic poet when he writes a poem, is a resurrection not just of human life but of life more generally—of a life which he images most often in vegetable life, as here with 'spinney'.

In the prose this dimension of meaning is hinted at only weakly by 'the spring'—'yet equally near him were the spring and Mary Magdalene and life'. It is given more substance in the section which follows, and closes Chapter Six, where we learn that during Zhivago's illness his half-brother has been constantly at his bedside and has talked to Tonya, urging her to retreat to the Urals:

I asked him what he thought, and he said it was a very good idea. We could grow vegetables and there's the forest all round. There isn't any point in dying without a struggle, like sheep.

But this has more to do with the poem called 'The Bad Days' than with either of the Magdalen poems. What is more to the point here is a reflection in the 13th section of Chapter Fifteen, on the behaviour of the flowers round Zhivago's coffin:

The kingdom of plants can easily be thought of as the nearest neighbour of the kingdom of death. Perhaps the mysteries of transformation and the enigmas of life which so torment us are concentrated in the green of the earth, among the trees in graveyards and the flowering shoots springing from their beds. Mary Magdalene, not at once recognizing Jesus risen from the grave, took Him for the gardener.

Notes to 'Gethsemane'

Coming as it does after the two poems on Magdalen, 'Gethsemane' can as little as those poems be considered a work of straightforward Christian piety. It is entirely possible, so far as I know, that Pasternak died a faithful son of his church; and among his last poems is one, 'In Hospital', which breathes a pure Christian devotion. But Zhivago is a different matter. Not only does he seem in the novel to embrace the noble but certainly heterodox faith of his uncle, the lapsed priest Nikolai Nikolaievich, but as a poet quite plainly Zhivago uses the Christian story as a myth, structural and archetypal, just as for instance Joyce uses the Odysseus story. The first poem in the sequence, 'Hamlet', a poem very explicitly echoed in the 6th stanza of 'Gethsemane', has established from the start that, whereas the Christian must believe the Christ-story unique and unrepeatable, Zhivago sees in it an archetypal pattern reproduced in the life of the tragic hero Hamlet and to some extent reproduced in his own life also. Lara sees herself at least once as standing in the same relation to Zhivago as the Magdalen does to Christ. And repeatedly Zhivago speaks of miracles, and wonder-working, with a careful ambiguity which has as much to do with the miracle of artistic creation as with the prodigies performed by Christ; indeed there is the same ambiguity about the very word, 'creation'. It is possible, though it would be perverse, to read all the overtly Christian poems in the sequence as celebrating the apotheosis of the heroic and martyred artist. All this surely invalidates Max Hayward's extraordinary observation (in *Encounter* for May 1958) that 'Zhivago is not a Jesus-like figure. He is more like an apostle, one of those disciples who could not keep awake during the vigil of Gethsemane . . .'

To be more specific, what Christ is made to say in the penultimate stanza of 'Gethsemane' seems to be quite blasphemously at odds with Christian dogma. Dogma holds, surely, that just as Christ when crucified escaped from time back into eternity, so the Crucifixion permits mortals who apprehend its significance similarly to escape the temporal dimension. Zhivago's Christ, on the contrary, goes to his crucifixion so as to be at one with the historical process, for the sake of something which works itself out wholly within time:

> See how the times turn allegorical,
> How they catch fire in very course of turning.
> In the name of the terror of their potency
> I seek the tomb in voluntary pains.

When he gives these words to Christ, Zhivago appears to be agreeing with Boris Pasternak not in the latter's Christianity but rather in what I call, not very happily perhaps, his apocalyptic Marxism. Christianity and historical determinism are perhaps reconcilable, though I think not without difficulty. In any case Pasternak, both when he writes as Zhivago and when he writes in his own character, seems to believe that at any given time there is a logic working itself out in historical events, and that no man lives so wisely and so well as he who has rightly divined whither history in his time is tending. And this is surely much nearer to a Marxist way of thinking than to the Christian way, since to the Christian one historical

156

event in the past, the Incarnation, alone gives meaning and dignity to history; and history of itself tends nowhither, unless to the Second Coming.

I must not seem to be denying that the Jesus in the poem is indeed the historical Jesus of the gospels; or to be maintaining that on the contrary in this poem Jesus is an allegory of Zhivago. If I read *Doctor Zhivago* aright, it is not at all an allegorical work, but symbolical. And I conceive that in such a work just as Mary Magdalene can indeed be Mary Magdalene, and yet also Lara, and other women too, so Jesus can be very fully and seriously Jesus, yet also Zhivago, and also other men besides Zhivago. If so it will be quite proper, and indeed necessary, to ask such questions as: who was Zhivago's Judas? who was Zhivago's Peter? who were his disciples?

If we start by looking for Judas, what we find points, not to Zhivago as the Christ-figure, but to quite another character, and a minor one.

> With fire and sword and in the forefront Judas
> With all the treacherous kissing in his lips . . .

What these lines recall is a moment in the 1st section of Chapter Twelve, 'Iced Rowanberries'. The commander of the Red partisans in the tayga has used Sivobluy, one of his bodyguard, as an *agent provocateur* so as to trap the mutineers in his force. Betrayed and convicted, they are now to suffer summary execution, and as they are herded towards the precipice where they are to be shot they scream at Sivobluy:

Judas! Christ-killer! If we are traitors, you are a traitor three times over, you dog, may you choke. You killed your lawful tsar to whom you took your oath, you swore loyalty to us and you betrayed us. Mind you kiss your devil, your Forester, before you betray him! You'll betray him all right!

Undoubtedly the force of this, and of the whole episode, is in the first place a triumph of realism, of verisimilitude: supposedly revolutionary heroes, the partisans employ against each other the most hated of all the strategies of the Tsarist secret police, the *agent provocateur*; and when they have nothing to lose they reveal themselves as still wholly Tsarist in sentiment. Compared with this, the symbolical significance is only secondary. Yet it is insistent. For the mutineers as a whole are a despicable rabble, yet they include two better men, the old anarchists Vdovichenko and Rzhanitsky. Rzhanitsky turns out to have secreted a revolver which, in a gesture of furious defiance, he fires three times at the partisans ('aiming at Sivobluy'); missing with all three shots he flings his revolver to the ground, whereupon 'It went off a fourth time, wounding one of the condemned men, the orderly Pachkolya, in the foot.' Here surely is the Peter-figure, wounding the orderly in the foot as Peter cuts off the ear of the high priest's servant.

This points to Rzhanitsky's associate, Vdovichenko, as the Christ-figure. And sure enough:

On the verge of the grave, Vdovichenko remained true to himself as he had been throughout his life. His head high, his grey hair streaming in the wind, he addressed Rzhanitsky as one *communard* to another, in a voice loud enough to be heard by all:

'Don't humble yourself! Your protest will not reach

them. These new *oprichniki*, these master craftsmen of the new torture chambers will never understand you! But don't lose heart. History will tell the truth. Posterity will nail the Bourbons of the commissarocracy to a pillar of shame, it will pillory their dark deeds. We die as martyrs at the dawn of the world revolution. Hail, revolution of the spirit! Hail, universal anarchy!'

Plainly, 'History will tell the truth' and 'Hail, universal anarchy!' are Vdovichenko's ways of saying,

> See how the times turn allegorical . . .
> In the name of the terror of their potency
> I seek the tomb in voluntary pains.

And yet Vdovichenko counts for nothing in the story, is a marginal character, one of the soonest forgotten.

Zhivago has no Judas. Nor has he any figure who plays Peter to his Christ, as plainly as Rzhanitsky plays Peter to Vdovichenko. But one might point to a Peter-figure in Vassya Brykin, the young conscript who vanishes from the novel when he escapes from the train which carries Zhivago to the Urals, only to reappear near the end when Zhivago, coming back from the Urals, meets him again in the charred ruins of his village and carries him along to Moscow. This is told in the 3rd and 4th sections of the Conclusion; in the 5th section we learn how Vassya learns printing and book-design, and so produces the books which Zhivago writes, but how after a while this disciple gradually deserts his master—

There came a time when the friendship between Yury and Vassya cooled. Vassya had developed remarkably. He no longer thought or spoke like the ragged, bare-footed, dishevelled boy from Veretenniki. The obviousness, the self-evidence of the truths proclaimed by the revolution attracted him increasingly, and Yury's talk, with its obscurities and its imagery, now struck him as the voice of error, doomed, conscious of its weakness and therefore evasive.

Yury was making calls on various government departments. He was trying to get two things: the political rehabilitation of his family and permission for them to return to Russia, as well as a foreign passport for himself and permission to fetch them from Paris.

Vassya was astonished at how lukewarm and half-hearted his efforts were. Yury seemed always to be in a hurry to believe that his efforts had failed; he spoke with too much conviction and almost with satisfaction of the futility of undertaking anything further.

Vassya's impatience with Zhivago's fatalism is surely like the state of mind in which Peter offered resistance to the mob when Jesus would not. And as Peter subsequently denied his master, so 'Vassya found fault with Yury more and more often and, although Yury did not take offence at being justly criticized, his relationship with Vassya gradually deteriorated. Finally their friendship broke up, and they parted company.' After this 'Yury gave up medicine, neglected himself, stopped seeing his friends and lived in great poverty'.

If Vassya Brykin is one of Zhivago's disciples, others are Misha Gordon and Nicky Dudorov, his boyhood friends who are entrusted with the epilogue in which we learn, twenty years after Zhivago's death, about the daughter he had by Lara. In a brilliantly realistic and penetrating passage (the 7th section of the Conclusion) we are shown how Gordon and Dudorov have had to do violence to themselves in order to come to terms with the regime. And Zhivago, at this point still alive in Moscow, perceives it also:

To Yury the springs of their emotion and of their reasoning and the shakiness of their sympathy were as clear as daylight. But he could hardly say to them: 'Dear friends, how desperately commonplace you are—you, your circle, the names and the authorities you quote, their brilliance and the art you so much admire! The only bright and living thing about you is that you are living at the same time as myself and are my friends!'—But how could anyone confess to such a thought? . . .

The answer is that Christ could confess to it when in 'Gethsemane' he says to his disciples who have failed him:

> You has the Lord appointed
> To live in my day . . .

There seems no room for doubt that when Zhivago gave these words to Christ he was voicing what he felt about Gordon and Dudorov.

What's more, in the next very brief section (the 8th), after Zhivago has disappeared, he writes to Gordon and Dudorov explaining that he has gone, as it were, into the garden to pray alone:

He told them that in order to rebuild his life as completely and rapidly as possible, he wished to spend some time by himself, concentrating on his affairs, and that as soon as he was settled in a job and reasonably certain of not falling back into his old ways, he would leave his hiding-place and return to Marina and the children.

This explanation constitutes his 'Tarry ye here, and watch with me'—a request which they do not honour, since they immediately try to hunt him down.

That he none the less evades them is miraculous—
'Yet all the time he was living within a stone's
throw, right under their eyes and noses, in the middle
of the district they were combing for him' (Section 9).
This is miraculous since, like all the other details of
Zhivago's retreat, it is contrived by the superhuman
agency of his half-brother Yevgraf. And my teasing
out of sometimes tenuous parallels will be justified if
it casts some light on this crucial and baffling figure,
elusive and invulnerable.

Edmund Wilson is certainly right to refuse to take
Yevgraf at his face value, as a realistic portrayal.[1]
Pasternak has gone out of his way to make this impossible, deliberately destroying verisimilitude whenever Yevgraf makes his sparse but always momentous
appearances, always as a *deus ex machina*. And plainly
too it is of very great significance that Yevgraf's name
in the Russian calendar means 'writer'. Mrs Lehovich,
Mr Wilson's collaborator, decides that 'Yevgraf is
Yury's creative genius'; and certainly this is very near
to the whole truth about him. Yet if there is any substance at all to my reading of 'Gethsemane', it must
appear that Yevgraf stands to Yuri Zhivago in the
same relation as God the Father to God the Son.
It is Yevgraf who could, who in the novel repeatedly
did, dispatch 'a myriad of winged legions' to save
Zhivago. This does not mean that he cannot be
'Yury's creative genius', but only that the nature of
genius and of inspiration must be understood a little
differently from Mr Wilson's understanding of it
when he writes of Yevgraf as 'Yury's *alter ego*, his

[1] Edmund Wilson, 'Legend and Symbol in "Doctor
Zhivago"'. *Encounter*, June 1959.

creative, his poetic self'. What we want is a conception of poetic creativity, not as a potentiality within the person, but as a force applied to him or descending upon him from outside his personality. And this is just what we find in the 8th section of Chapter Fourteen, when Zhivago is writing his poems:

After two or three stanzas and several images by which he was himself astonished, his work took possession of him and he experienced the approach of what is called inspiration. At such moments the correlation of the forces controlling the artist is, as it were, stood on its head. The ascendancy is no longer with the artist or the state of mind which he is trying to express, but with language, his instrument of expression. Language, the home and dwelling of beauty and meaning, itself begins to think and speak for man and turns wholly into music, not in the sense of outward, audible sounds but by virtue of the power and momentum of its inward flow. Then, like the current of a mighty river polishing stones and turning wheels by its very movement, the flow of speech creates in passing, by the force of its own laws, rhyme and rhythm and countless other forms and formations, still more important and until now undiscovered, unconsidered and unnamed.

At such moments Yury felt that the main part of his work was not being done by him but by something which was above him and controlling him: the thought and poetry of the world as it was at that moment and as it would be in the future. He was controlled by the next step it was to take in the order of its historical development; and he felt himself to be only the pretext and the pivot setting it in motion.

(Here again, in the last sentences, one notes the apocalyptic Marxism—if this is what Yevgraf is, and if he is also God the Father, it is a God who does not transcend history but on the contrary is a force within history, manifest only in the turnings round of time. It is not for nothing, perhaps, that Yevgraf's last manifestation is as a General of the Red Army in the second world war.) I conclude that Yevgraf is indeed Yury Zhivago's creative genius, but a genius seen as inhering not in the artist, but in his art and the medium of his art. That medium is language. But as the penultimate sentence makes clear, it is not narrowly the Russian language. Yevgraf is not the genius of the Russian language, nor of the Russian literary tradition; he is the genius of all language, and of the world's literature seen as a whole. After all, it could hardly be otherwise: if Yevgraf is to take the weight which the work as a whole requires him to take, he cannot be a personal, nor a national, nor even narrowly a human potency. What he must and does represent (he cannot be said to embody it, for he is not sufficiently 'present') is the creative potency of language considered as a natural force like wind or water.

THE POEMS IN THE
ORIGINAL RUSSIAN

СТИХОТВОРЕНИЯ ЮРИЯ ЖИВАГО

1

Г А М Л Е Т

Гул затих. Я вышел на подмостки.
Прислонясь к дверному косяку,
Я ловлю в далеком отголоске
Что случится на моем веку.

На меня наставлен сумрак ночи
Тысячью биноклей на оси.
Если только можно, Авва Отче,
Чашу эту мимо пронеси.

Я люблю Твой замысел упрямый
И играть согласен эту роль.
Но сейчас идет другая драма,
И на этот раз меня уволь.

Но продуман распорядок действий,
И неотвратим конец пути.
Я, один, всё тонет в фарисействе.
Жизнь прожить — не поле перейти.

2

М А Р Т

Солнце греет до седьмого пота,
И бушует, одурев, овраг.
Как у дюжей скотницы работа,
Дело у весны кипит в руках.

Чахнет снег и болен малокровьем
В веточках бессильно синих жил.
Но дымится жизнь в хлеву коровьем,
И здоровьем пышут зубья вил.

Эти ночи, эти дни и ночи!
Дробь капелей к середине дня,
Кровельных сосулек худосочье,
Ручейков бессонных болтовня!

Настежь всё, конюшня и коровник.
Голуби в снегу клюют овес,
И всего живитель и виновник, —
Пахнет свежим воздухом навоз.

3

НА СТРАСТНОЙ

Еще кругом ночная мгла.
Еще так рано в мире,
Что звездам в небе нет числа,
И каждая, как день, светла,
И если бы земля могла,
Она бы Пасху проспала
Под чтение Псалтыри.

Еще кругом ночная мгла.
Такая рань на свете,
Что площадь вечностью легла
От перекрестка до угла,
И до рассвета и тепла
Еще тысячелетье.

Еще земля голым-гола,
И ей ночами не в чем
Раскачивать колокола
И вторить с воли певчим.

И со Страстного четверга
Вплоть до Страстной субботы
Вода буравит берега
И вьет водовороты.

И лес раздет и непокрыт,
И на Страстях Христовых,
Как строй молящихся, стоит
Толпой стволов сосновых.

А в городе, на небольшом
Пространстве, как на сходке,
Деревья смотрят нагишом
В церковные решетки.

И взгляд их ужасом объят.
Понятна их тревога.
Сады выходят из оград,
Колеблется земли уклад:
Они хоронят Бога.

И видят свет у царских врат,
И черный плат, и свечек ряд,
Заплаканные лица —
И вдруг навстречу крестный ход
Выходит с плащаницей,
И две березы у ворот
Должны посторониться.

И шествие обходит двор
По краю тротуара,
И вносит с улицы в притвор
Весну, весенний разговор,
И воздух с привкусом просфор
И вешнего угара.

И март разбрасывает снег
На паперти толпе калек,

Как-будто вышел человек,
И вынес, и открыл ковчег,
И всё до нитки роздал.

И пенье длится до зари,
И, нарыдавшись вдосталь,
Доходят тише изнутри
На пустыри под фонари
Псалтырь или Апостол.

Но в полночь смолкнут тварь и плоть,
Заслышав слух весенний,
Что только-только распогодь,
Смерть можно будет побороть
Усильем Воскресенья.

4

БЕЛАЯ НОЧЬ

Мне далекое время мерещится,
Дом на Стороне Петербургской.
Дочь степной небогатой помещицы,
Ты — на курсах, ты родом из Курска.

Ты — мила, у тебя есть поклонники.
Этой белою ночью мы оба,
Примостясь на твоем подоконнике,
Смотрим вниз с твоего небоскреба.

Фонари, точно бабочки газовые,
Утро тронуло первою дрожью.
То, что тихо тебе я рассказываю,
Так на спящие дали похоже.

Мы охвачены тою же самою
Оробелою верностью тайне,

Как раскинувшийся панорамою
Петербург за Невою бескрайней.

Там вдали, по дремучим урочищам,
Этой ночью весеннею белой,
Соловьи славословьем грохочущим
Оглашают лесные пределы.

Ошалелое щелканье катится,
Голос маленькой птички ледащей
Пробуждает восторг и сумятицу
В глубине очарованной чащи.

В те места босоногою странницей
Пробирается ночь вдоль забора
И за ней с подоконника тянется
След подслушанного разговора.

В отголосках беседы услышанной
По садам, огороженным тесом,
Ветви яблоновые и вишенные
Одеваются цветом белесым.

И деревья, как призраки, белые
Высыпают толпой на дорогу,
Точно знаки прощальные делая
Белой ночи, видавшей так много.

5

ВЕСЕННЯЯ РАСПУТИЦА

Огни заката догорали.
Распутицей в бору глухом
В далекий хутор на Урале
Тащился человек верхом.

М

Болтала лошадь селезенкой
И звону шлепавших подков
Дорогой вторила вдогонку
Вода в воронках родников.

Когда же опускал поводья
И шагом ехал верховой,
Прокатывало половодье
Вблизи весь гул и грохот свой.

Смеялся кто-то, плакал кто-то,
Крошились камни о кремни,
И падали.в водовороты
С корнями вырванные пни.

А на пожарище заката,
В далекой прочерни ветвей,
Как гулкий колокол набата
Неистовствовал соловей.

Где ива вдовий свой повойник
Клонила, свесивши в овраг,
Как древний соловей-разбойник
Свистал он на семи дубах.

Какой беде, какой зазнобе
Предназначался этот пыл?
В кого ружейной крупной дробью
Он по чащобе запустил?

Казалось, вот он выйдет лешим
С привала беглых каторжан
Навстречу конным или пешим
Заставам здешних партизан.

Земля и небо, лес и поле
Ловили этот редкий звук,
Размеренные эти доли
Безумья, боли, счастья, мук.

6

ОБЪЯСНЕНИЕ

Жизнь вернулась так же беспричинно,
Как когда-то странно прервалась.
Я на той же улице старинной,
Как тогда, в тот летний день и час.

Те же люди и заботы те же,
И пожар заката не остыл,
Как его тогда к стене Манежа
Вечер смерти наспех пригвоздил.

Женщины в дешевом затрапезе
Так же ночью топчут башмаки.
Их потом на кровельном железе
Так же распинают чердаки.

Вот одна походкою усталой
Медленно выходит на порог
И, поднявшись из полуподвала,
Переходит двор наискосок.

Я опять готовлю отговорки,
И опять всё безразлично мне.
И соседка, обогнув задворки,
Оставляет нас наедине.

————————

Не плачь, не морщь опухших губ,
Не собирай их в складки.
Разбередишь присохший струп
Весенней лихорадки.

Сними ладонь с моей груди,
Мы провода под током.

Друг к другу вновь, того гляди,
Нас бросит ненароком.

Пройдут года, ты вступишь в брак,
Забудешь неустройства.
Быть женщиной — великий шаг,
Сводить с ума — геройство.

А я пред чудом женских рук,
Спины, и плеч, и шеи
И так с привязанностью слуг
Весь век благоговею.

Но как ни сковывает ночь
Меня кольцом тоскливым,
Сильней на свете тяга прочь
И манит страсть к разрывам.

7

ЛЕТО В ГОРОДЕ

Разговоры вполголоса
И с поспешностью пылкой
Кверху собраны волосы
Всей копною с затылка.

Из-под гребня тяжелого
Смотрит женщина в шлеме,
Запрокинувши голову
Вместе с косами всеми.

А на улице жаркая
Ночь сулит непогоду,
И расходятся, шаркая,
По домам пешеходы.

Гром отрывистый слышится,
Отдающийся резко,

И от ветра колышится
На окне занавеска.

Наступает безмолвие,
Но попрежнему парит,
И попрежнему молнии
В небе шарят и шарят.

А когда светозарное
Утро знойное снова
Сушит лужи бульварные
После ливня ночного,

Смотрят хмуро по случаю
Своего недосыпа
Вековые, пахучие,
Неотцветшие липы.

8

ВЕТЕР

Я кончился, а ты жива.
И ветер, жалуясь и плача,
Раскачивает лес и дачу.
Не каждую сосну отдельно,
А полностью все дерева
Со всею далью беспредельной,
Как парусников кузова
На глади бухты корабельной.
И это не из удальства
Или из ярости бесцельной,
А чтоб в тоске найти слова
Тебе для песни колыбельной.

9

ХМЕЛЬ

Под ракитой, обвитой плющом,
От ненастья мы ищем защиты.
Наши плечи покрыты плащом,
Вкруг тебя мои руки обвиты.

Я ошибся. Кусты этих чащ
Не плющом перевиты, а хмелем.
Ну так лучше давай этот плащ
В ширину под собою расстелем.

10

БАБЬЕ ЛЕТО

Лист смородины груб и матерчат.
В доме хохот и стекла звенят,
В нем шинкуют, и квасят, и перчат,
И гвоздики кладут в маринад.

Лес забрасывает, как насмешник,
Этот шум на обрывистый склон,
Где сгоревший на солнце орешник,
Словно жаром костра опален.

Здесь дорога спускается в балку,
Здесь и высохших старых коряг,
И лоскутницы осени жалко,
Всё сметающей в этот овраг.

И того, что вселенная проще,
Чем иной полагает хитрец,
Что как в воду опущена роща,
Что приходит всему свой конец.

Что глазами бессмысленно хлопать,
Когда всё пред тобой сожжено,
И осенняя белая копоть
Паутиною тянет в окно.

Ход из сада в заборе проломан
И теряется в березняке.
В доме смех и хозяйственный гомон,
Тот же гомон и смех вдалеке.

11

СВАДЬБА

Пересекши край двора,
Гости на гулянку
В дом невесты до утра
Перешли с тальянкой.

За хозяйскими дверьми
В войлочной обивке
Стихли с часу до семи
Болтовни обрывки.

А зарею, в самый сон,
Только спать и спать бы,
Вновь запел акордеон,
Уходя со свадьбы.

И рассыпал гармонист
Снова на баяне
Плеск ладоней, блеск монист,
Шум и гам гулянья.

И опять, опять, опять
Говорок частушки
Прямо к спящим на кровать
Ворвался с пирушки.

А одна, как снег, бела,
В шуме, свисте, гаме
Снова павой поплыла,
Поводя боками,

Помавая головой
И рукою правой,
В плясовой по мостовой,
Павой, павой, павой.

Вдруг задор и шум игры,
Топот хоровода,
Провалясь в тартарары,
Канули, как в воду.

Просыпался шумный двор.
Деловое эхо
Вмешивалось в разговор
И раскаты смеха.

В необъятность неба, ввысь
Вихрем сизых пятен
Стаей голуби неслись,
Снявшись с голубятен.

Точно их за свадьбой вслед
Спохватясь спросонья,
С пожеланьем многих лет
Выслали в погоню.

Жизнь ведь тоже только миг,
Только растворенье
Нас самих во всех других
Как бы им в даренье.

Только свадьба, вглубь окон
Рвущаяся снизу,
Только песня, только сон,
Только голубь сизый.

12

ОСЕНЬ

Я дал разъехаться домашним,
Все близкие давно в разброде,
И одиночеством всегдашним
Полно всё в сердце и природе.

И вот я здесь с тобой в сторожке,
В лесу безлюдно и пустынно.
Как в песне, стежки и дорожки
Позаросли наполовину.

Теперь на нас одних с печалью
Глядят бревенчатые стены.
Мы брать преград не обещали,
Мы будем гибнуть откровенно.

Мы сядем в час и встанем в третьем,
Я с книгою, ты с вышиваньем,
И на рассвете не заметим,
Как целоваться перестанем.

Еще пышней и бесшабашней
Шумите, осыпайтесь, листья,
И чашу горечи вчерашней
Сегодняшней тоской превысьте.

Привязанность, влеченье, прелесть!
Рассеемся в сентябрьском шуме!
Заройся вся в осенний шелест!
Замри, или ополоумей!

Ты так же сбрасываешь платье,
Как роща сбрасывает листья,
Когда ты падаешь в объятье
В халате с шелковою кистью.

Ты — благо гибельного шага,
Когда житье тошней недуга,
А корень красоты — отвага,
И это тянет нас друг к другу.

13

СКАЗКА

Встарь, во время оно,
В сказочном краю
Пробирался конный
Степью по репью.

Он спешил на сечу,
А в степной пыли
Темный лес навстречу
Вырастал вдали.

Ныло ретивое,
На сердце скребло:
Бойся водопоя,
Подтяни седло.

Не послушал конный
И во весь опор
Залетел с разгону
На лесной бугор.

Повернул с кургана,
Въехал в суходол,
Миновал поляну,
Гору перешел.

И забрел в ложбину
И лесной тропой
Вышел на звериный
След и водопой.

И глухой к призыву,
И не вняв чутью,
Свел коня с обрыва
Попоить к ручью.

———————

У ручья пещера,
Пред пещерой — брод.
Как бы пламя серы
Озаряло вход.

И в дыму багровом,
Застилавшем взор,
Отдаленным зовом
Огласился бор.

И тогда оврагом,
Вздрогнув, напрямик
Тронул конный шагом
На призывный крик.

И увидел конный,
И приник к копью,
Голову дракона,
Хвост и чешую.

Пламенем из зева
Рассевал он свет,
В три кольца вкруг девы
Обмотав хребет.

Туловище змея,
Как концом бича,
Поводило шеей
У ее плеча.

Той страны обычай
Пленницу-красу
Отдавал в добычу
Чудищу в лесу.

Края населенье
Хижины свои
Выкупало пеней
Этой от змеи.

Змей обвил ей руку
И оплел гортань,
Получив на муку
В жертву эту дань.

Посмотрел с мольбою
Всадник в высь небес
И копье для боя
Взял на перевес.

———————

Сомкнутые веки.
Выси. Облака.
Воды. Броды. Реки.
Годы и века.

Конный в шлеме сбитом,
Сшибленный в бою.
Верный конь, копытом
Топчущий змею.

Конь и труп дракона
Рядом на песке.
В обмороке конный,
Дева в столбняке.

Светел свод полдневный,
Синева нежна.
Кто она? Царевна?
Дочь земли? Княжна?

То, в избытке счастья
Слезы в три ручья,
То душа во власти
Сна и забытья.

То возврат здоровья,
То недвижность жил
От потери крови
И упадка сил.

Но сердца их бьются.
То она, то он
Силятся очнуться
И впадают в сон.

Сомкнутые веки.
Выси. Облака.
Воды. Броды. Реки.
Годы и века.

14

АВГУСТ

Как обещало, не обманывая,
Проникло солнце утром рано
Косою полосой шафрановою
От занавеси до дивана.

Оно покрыло жаркой охрою
Соседний лес, дома поселка,
Мою постель, подушку мокрую
И край стены за книжной полкой.

Я вспомнил, по какому поводу
Слегка увлажнена подушка.
Мне снилось, что ко мне на проводы,
Шли по лесу вы друг за дружкой.

Вы шли толпою, врозь и парами,
Вдруг кто-то вспомнил, что сегодня
Шестое августа по старому,
Преображение Господне.

Обыкновенно свет без пламени
Исходит в этот день с Фавора,
И осень, ясная как знаменье,
К себе приковывает взоры.

И вы прошли сквозь мелкий, нищенский,
Нагой, трепещущий ольшаник
В имбирно-красный лес кладбищенский,
Горевший, как печатный пряник.

С притихшими его вершинами
Соседствовало небо важно,
И голосами петушиными
Перекликалась даль протяжно.

В лесу казенной землемершею
Стояла смерть среди погоста,
Смотря в лицо мое умершее,
Чтоб вырыть яму мне по росту.

Был всеми ощутим физически
Спокойный голос чей-то рядом.
То прежний голос мой провидческий
Звучал, нетронутый распадом:

«Прощай, лазурь преображенская
И золото второго Спаса.
Смягчи последней лаской женскою
Мне горечь рокового часа.

Прощайте, годы безвременщины.
Простимся, бездне унижений
Бросающая вызов женщина!
Я — поле твоего сраженья.

Прощай, размах крыла расправленный,
Полета вольное упорство,
И образ мира, в слове явленный,
И творчество, и чудотворство».

15

ЗИМНЯЯ НОЧЬ

Мело, мело по всей земле
Во все пределы.
Свеча горела на столе,
Свеча горела.

Как летом роем мошкара
Летит на пламя,
Слетались хлопья со двора
К оконной раме.

Метель лепила на стекле
Кружки и стрелы.
Свеча горела на столе,
Свеча горела.

На озаренный потолок
Ложились тени,
Скрещенья рук, скрещенья ног,
Судьбы скрещенья.

И падали два башмачка
Со стуком на пол.
И воск слезами с ночника
На платье капал.

И всё терялось в снежной мгле
Седой и белой.
Свеча горела на столе,
Свеча горела.

На свечку дуло из угла,
И жар соблазна
Вздымал, как ангел, два крыла
Крестообразно.

Мело весь месяц в феврале,
И то и дело
Свеча горела на столе,
Свеча горела.

16

РАЗЛУКА

С порога смотрит человек,
Не узнавая дома.
Ее отъезд был как побег.
Везде следы разгрома.

Повсюду в комнатах хаос.
Он меры разоренья
Не замечает из-за слез
И приступа мигрени.

В ушах с утра какой-то шум.
Он в памяти иль грезит?
И почему ему на ум
Всё мысль о море лезет?

Когда сквозь иней на окне
Не видно света божья,
Безвыходность тоски вдвойне
С пустыней моря схожа.

Она была так дорога
Ему чертой любою,
Как морю близки берега
Всей линией прибоя.

Как затопляет камыши
Волненье после шторма,
Ушли на дно его души
Ее черты и формы.

В года мытарств, во времена
Немыслимого быта
Она волной судьбы со дна
Была к нему прибита.

Среди препятствий без числа,
Опасности минуя,
Волна несла ее, несла
И пригнала вплотную.

И вот теперь ее отъезд,
Насильственный, быть может
Разлука их обоих съест,
Тоска с костями сгложет.

И человек глядит кругом:
Она в момент ухода
Всё выворотила вверх дном
Из ящиков комода.

Он бродит, и до темноты
Укладывает в ящик
Раскиданные лоскуты
И выкройки образчик.

И наколовшись об шитье
С невынутой иголкой,
Внезапно видит всю ее
И плачет втихомолку.

17

СВИДАНИЕ

Засыпет снег дороги,
Завалит скаты крыш.
Пойду размять я ноги:
За дверью ты стоишь.

187

Одна в пальто осеннем,
Без шляпы, без калош,
Ты борешься с волненьем
И мокрый снег жуешь.

Деревья и ограды
Уходят вдаль, во мглу.
Одна средь снегопада
Стоишь ты на углу.

Течет вода с косынки
За рукава в обшлаг,
И каплями росинки
Сверкают в волосах.

И прядью белокурой
Озарены: лицо,
Косынка и фигура
И это пальтецо.

Снег на ресницах влажен,
В твоих глазах тоска,
И весь твой облик слажен
Из одного куска.

Как будто бы железом,
Обмокнутым в сурьму
Тебя вели нарезом
По сердцу моему.

И в нем навек засело
Смиренье этих черт,
И оттого нет дела,
Что свет жестокосерд.

И оттого двоится
Вся эта ночь в снегу,
И провести границы
Меж нас я не могу.

Но кто мы и откуда,
Когда от всех тех лет
Остались пересуды,
А нас на свете нет?

18

РОЖДЕСТВЕНСКАЯ ЗВЕЗДА

Стояла зима.
Дул ветер из степи.
И холодно было Младенцу в вертепе
На склоне холма.

Его согревало дыханье вола.
Домашние звери
Стояли в пещере,
Над яслями теплая дымка плыла.

Доху отряхнув от постельной трухи
И зернышек проса,
Смотрели с утеса
Спросонья в полночную даль пастухи.

Вдали было поле в снегу и погост,
Ограды, надгробья,
Оглобля в сугробе,
И небо над кладбищем, полное звезд.

А рядом, неведомая перед тем,
Застенчивей плошки
В оконце сторожки
Мерцала звезда по пути в Вифлеем.

Она пламенела, как стог, в стороне
От неба и Бога,
Как отблеск поджога,
Как хутор в огне и пожар на гумне.

Она возвышалась горящей скирдой
Соломы и сена
Средь целой вселенной,
Встревоженной этою новой звездой.

Растущее зарево рдело над ней
И значило что-то,
И три звездочета
Спешили на зов небывалых огней.

За ними везли на верблюдах дары.
И ослики в сбруе, один малорослей
Другого, шажками спускались с горы.

И странным виденьем грядущей поры
Вставало вдали всё пришедшее после.
Все мысли веков, все мечты, все миры,
Всё будущее галерей и музеев,
Все шалости фей, все дела чародеев,
Все елки на свете, все сны детворы.

Весь трепет затепленных свечек, все цепи,
Всё великолепье цветной мишуры...
...Всё злей и свирепей дул ветер из степи..
...Все яблоки, все золотые шары.

Часть пруда скрывали верхушки ольхи,
Но часть было видно отлично отсюда
Сквозь гнезда грачей и деревьев верхи.
Как шли вдоль запруды ослы и верблюды,
Могли хорошо разглядеть пастухи.
— Пойдемте со всеми, поклонимся чуду, —
Сказали они, запахнув кожухи.

От шарканья по снегу сделалось жарко.
По яркой поляне листами слюды
Вели за хибарку босые следы.
На эти следы, как на пламя огарка,
Ворчали овчарки при свете звезды.

Морозная ночь походила на сказку,
И кто-то с навьюженной снежной гряды
Всё время незримо входил в их ряды.
Собаки брели, озираясь с опаской,
И жались к подпаску, и ждали беды.

По той же дороге, чрез эту же местность
Шло несколько ангелов в гуще толпы.
Незримыми делала их бестелесность,
Но шаг оставлял отпечаток стопы.

У камня толпилась орава народу.
Светало. Означились кедров стволы.
— А кто вы такие? — спросила Мария.
— Мы племя пастушье и неба послы,
Пришли вознести вам обоим хвалы.
— Всем вместе нельзя. Подождите у входа.

Средь серой, как пепел, предутренней мглы
Топтались погонщики и овцеводы,
Ругались со всадниками пешеходы,
У выдолбленной водопойной колоды
Ревели верблюды, лягались ослы.

Светало. Рассвет, как пылинки золы,
Последние звезды сметал с небосвода.
И только волхвов из несметного сброда
Впустила Мария в отверстье скалы.

Он спал, весь сияющий, в яслях из дуба,
Как месяца луч, в углубленье дупла.
Ему заменяли овчинную шубу
Ослиные губы и ноздри вола.

Стояли в тени, словно в сумраке хлева,
Шептались, едва подбирая слова.
Вдруг кто-то в потемках, немного налево
От яслей рукой отодвинул волхва,
И тот оглянулся: с порога на деву
Как гостья, смотрела звезда Рождества.

191

19

РАССВЕТ

Ты значил всё в моей судьбе.
Потом пришла война, разруха
И долго-долго о тебе
Ни слуху не было, ни духу.

И через много-много лет
Твой голос вновь меня встревожил.
Всю ночь читал я твой завет
И как от обморока ожил.

Мне к людям хочется, в толпу,
В их утреннее оживленье.
Я всё готов разнесть в щепу
И всех поставить на колени.

И я по лестнице бегу,
Как будто выхожу впервые
На эти улицы в снегу
И вымершие мостовые.

Везде встают, огни, уют,
Пьют чай, торопятся к трамваям.
В теченье нескольких минут
Вид города неузнаваем.

В воротах вьюга вяжет сеть
Из густо падающих хлопьев,
И чтобы во-время поспеть,
Все мчатся недоев-недопив.

Я чувствую за них за всех,
Как будто побывал в их шкуре,
Я таю сам, как тает снег,
Я сам, как утро, брови хмурю.

Со мною люди без имен,
Деревья, дети, домоседы.
Я ими всеми побежден,
И только в том моя победа.

20

ЧУДО

Он шел из Вифании в Ерусалим,
Заранее грустью предчувствий томим.

Колючий кустарник на круче был выжжен,
Над хижиной ближней не двигался дым,
Был воздух горяч и камыш неподвижен,
И Мертвого моря покой недвижим.

И в горечи, спорившей с горечью моря,
Он шел с небольшою толпой облаков
По пыльной дороге на чье-то подворье,
Шел в город на сборище учеников.

И так углубился Он в мысли свои,
Что поле в унынье запахло полынью.
Всё стихло. Один Он стоял посредине,
А местность лежала пластом в забытьи.
Всё перемешалось: теплынь и пустыня,
И ящерицы, и ключи, и ручьи.

Смоковница высилась невдалеке,
Совсем без плодов, только ветки да листья.
И Он ей сказал: «Для какой ты корысти?
Какая мне радость в твоем столбняке?

Я жажду и алчу, а ты — пустоцвет,
И встреча с тобой безотрадней гранита.
О, как ты обидна и недаровита!
Останься такой до скончания лет».

По дереву дрожь осужденья прошла,
Как молнии искра по громоотводу,
Смоковницу испепелило до тла.

Найдись в это время минута свободы
У листьев, ветвей, и корней, и ствола,
Успели б вмешаться законы природы.
Но чудо есть чудо, и чудо есть Бог.
Когда мы в смятенье, тогда средь разброда
Оно настигает мгновенно, врасплох.

21

 З Е М Л Я

В московские особняки
Врывается весна нахрапом.
Выпархивает моль за шкапом
И ползает по летним шляпам,
И прячут шубы в сундуки.

По деревянным антресолям
Стоят цветочные горшки
С левкоем и желтофиолем,
И дышат комнаты привольем,
И пахнут пылью чердаки.

И улица за панибрата
С оконницей подслеповатой,
И белой ночи и закату
Не разминуться у реки.

И можно слышать в коридоре,
Что происходит на просторе,
О чем в случайном разговоре
С капелью говорит апрель.
Он знает тысячи историй

Про человеческое горе,
И по заборам стынут зори,
И тянут эту канитель.

И та же смесь огня и жути
На воле и в жилом уюте,
И всюду воздух сам не свой.
И тех же верб сквозные прутья
И тех же белых почек вздутья
И на окне, и на распутье,
На улице и в мастерской.

Зачем же плачет даль в тумане,
И горько пахнет перегной?
На то ведь и мое призванье,
Чтоб не скучали расстоянья,
Чтобы за городскою гранью
Земле не тосковать одной.

Для этого весною ранней
Со мною сходятся друзья,
И наши вечера — прощанья,
Пирушки наши — завещанья,
Чтоб тайная струя страданья
Согрела холод бытия.

22

ДУРНЫЕ ДНИ

Когда на последней неделе
Входил Он в Иерусалим,
Осанны навстречу гремели,
Бежали с ветвями за Ним.

195

А дни всё грозней и суровей,
Любовью не тронуть сердец,
Презрительно сдвинуты брови,
И вот послесловье, конец.

Свинцовою тяжестью всею
Легли на дворы небеса.
Искали улик фарисеи,
Юля перед ним, как лиса.

И темными силами храма
Он отдан подонкам на суд,
И с пылкостью тою же самой,
Как славили прежде, клянут.

Толпа на соседнем участке
Заглядывала из ворот,
Толклись в ожиданье развязки
И тыкались взад и вперед.

И полз шопоток по соседству,
И слухи со многих сторон.
И бегство в Египет и детство
Уже вспоминались, как сон.

Припомнился скат величавый
В пустыне, и та крутизна,
С которой всемирной державой
Его соблазнял Сатана.

И брачное пиршество в Кане,
И чуду дивящийся стол,
И море, которым в тумане
Он к лодке, как по суху, шел.

И сборище бедных в лачуге,
И спуск со свечою в подвал,
Где вдруг она гасла в испуге,
Когда воскрешенный вставал...

196

23

МАГДАЛИНА

I

Чуть ночь, мой демон тут как тут,
За прошлое моя расплата.
Придут и сердце мне сосут
Воспоминания разврата,
Когда, раба мужских причуд,
Была я дурой бесноватой
И улицей был мой приют.

Осталось несколько минут,
И тишь наступит гробовая.
Но раньше, чем они пройдут,
Я жизнь свою, дойдя до края,
Как алавастровый сосуд,
Перед Тобою разбиваю.

О, где бы я теперь была,
Учитель мой и мой Спаситель,
Когда б ночами у стола
Меня бы вечность не ждала,
Как новый, в сети ремесла
Мной завлеченный посетитель.

Но объясни, что значит грех
И смерть и ад, и пламень серный,
Когда я на глазах у всех
С Тобой, как с деревом побег,
Сраслась в своей тоске безмерной.

Когда Твои стопы, Исус,
Оперши о свои колени,
Я, может, обнимать учусь
Креста четырехгранный брус
И, чувств лишаясь, к телу рвусь,
Тебя готовя к погребенью.

24

МАГДАЛИНА

II

У людей пред праздником уборка.
В стороне от этой толчеи,
Обмываю миром из ведерка
Я стопы пречистые Твои.

Шарю и не нахожу сандалий.
Ничего не вижу из-за слез.
На глаза мне пеленой упали
Пряди распустившихся волос.

Ноги я Твои в подол уперла,
Их слезами облила, Исус,
Ниткой бус их обмотала с горла,
В волосы зарыла, как в бурнус.

Будущее вижу так подробно,
Словно Ты его остановил.
Я сейчас предсказывать способна
Вещим ясновиденьем сивилл.

Завтра упадет завеса в храме,
Мы в кружок собьемся в стороне,
И земля качнется под ногами,
Может быть, из жалости ко мне.

Перестроятся ряды конвоя,
И начнется всадников разъезд.
Словно в бурю смерч, над головою
Будет к небу рваться этот крест.

Брошусь на землю у ног Распятья,
Обомру и закушу уста.
Слишком многим руки для объятья
Ты раскинешь по концам креста.

Для кого на свете столько шири,
Столько муки и такая мощь?
Есть ли столько душ и жизней в мире?
Столько поселений, рек и рощ?

Но пройдут такие трое суток
И столкнут в такую пустоту,
Что за этот страшный промежуток
Я до Воскресенья дорасту.

25

ГЕФСИМАНСКИЙ САД

Мерцаньем звезд далеких безразлично
Был поворот дороги озарен.
Дорога шла вокруг горы Масличной,
Внизу под нею протекал Кедрон.

Лужайка обрывалась с половины.
За нею начинался Млечный путь.
Седые серебристые маслины
Пытались вдаль по воздуху шагнуть.

В конце был чей-то сад, надел земельный.
Учеников оставив за стеной,
Он им сказал: «Душа скорбит смертельно,
Побудьте здесь и бодрствуйте со Мной».

Он отказался без противоборства,
Как от вещей, полученных взаймы,
От всемогущества и чудотворства,
И был теперь, как смертные, как мы.

Ночная даль теперь казалась краем
Уничтоженья и небытия.
Простор вселенной был необитаем,
И только сад был местом для житья.

И, глядя в эти черные провалы,
Пустые, без начала и конца,
Чтоб эта чаша смерти миновала,
В поту кровавом Он молил Отца.

И лишь сказал, неведомо откуда
Толпа рабов и скопище бродяг,
Огни, мечи и впереди — Иуда
С предательским лобзаньем на устах.

Петр дал мечом отпор головорезам
И ухо одному из них отсек.
Но слышит: «Спор нельзя решать железом,
Вложи свой меч на место, человек.

Он разбудил их: «Вас Господь сподобил
Жить в дни Мои, вы ж разлеглись, как пласт.
Час Сына Человеческого пробил.
Он в руки грешников Себя предаст».

Смягчив молитвой смертную истому,
Он вышел за ограду. На земле
Ученики, осиленные дремой,
Валялись в придорожном ковыле.

Неужто тьмы крылатых легионов
Отец не снарядил бы Мне сюда?
И, волоска тогда на Мне не тронув,
Враги рассеялись бы без следа.

Но книга жизни подошла к странице,
Которая дороже всех святынь.
Сейчас должно написанное сбыться,
Пускай же сбудется оно. Аминь.

Ты видишь, ход веков подобен притче
И может загореться на ходу.

Во имя страшного ее величья
Я в добровольных муках в гроб сойду.

Я в гроб сойду и в третий день восстану,
И, как сплавляют по реке плоты,
Ко Мне на суд, как баржи каравана,
Столетья поплывут из темноты».

INDEX